MELBOURNE SYMPOSIUM
ON SEPTUAGINT LEXICOGRAPHY

SOCIETY OF BIBLICAL LITERATURE
SEPTUAGINT AND COGNATE STUDIES SERIES

Series Editors
Claude E. Cox
William Adler

Editorial Advisory Committee

N. Fernández Marcos, Madrid
M. Mulder, Leiden
I. Soisalon - Soininen, Helsinki
E. Tov, Jerusalem

Number 28

MELBOURNE SYMPOSIUM
ON SEPTUAGINT LEXICOGRAPHY

Takamitsu Muraoka, editor

MELBOURNE SYMPOSIUM ON SEPTUAGINT LEXICOGRAPHY

Edited by
Takamitsu Muraoka

Scholars Press
Atlanta, Georgia

MELBOURNE SYMPOSIUM ON SEPTUAGINT LEXICOGRAPHY

Takamitsu Muraoka, editor

© 1990
Society of Biblical Literature

Library of Congress Cataloging-in-Publication Data

Melbourne Symposium on Septuagint and Lexicography (1987 : University of Melbourne)
  Melbourne Symposium on Septuagint and Lexicography / edited by Takamitsu Muraoka.
  p. cm. -- (Septuagint and cognate studies series ; no. 28)
  ISBN 1-55540-486-3. -- ISBN 1-55540-487-1 (pbk.)
  1. Greek language, Biblical--Lexicography--Congresses. 2. Bible. O.T. Greek--Versions--Septuagint--Congresses. I. Muraoka, T. II. Title. III. Series.
PA781.M45 1987
487'.4--dc20   90-39741
                                                    CIP

Printed in the United States of America
on acid-free paper

TABLE OF CONTENTS   v

Introduction by the Editor   vii
    T. Muraoka (University of Melbourne)

Abbreviations   xv

συνίστημι: A sample lexical entry   1-16
    J.A.L. Lee (University of Sydney)

Septuagintal lexicography: some general issues   17-48
    T. Muraoka (University of Melbourne)

ἀγαπᾶν in the Septuagint   49-82
    S.P. Swinn (University of Macquarie)

"Greek words and Hebrew meanings"   83-126
    E. Tov (The Hebrew University, Jerusalem)

Indexes   127-136

    Biblical and other references

    Greek words

    Hebrew words

    Modern authors

INTRODUCTION BY THE EDITOR

Takamitsu Muraoka

The Bulletin no. 2 (p. 4) for the year 1969 of the International Organization for Septuagint and Cognate Studies (*BIOSCS*) refers to the possibility mooted of the IOSCS involved in the production of a new Septuagint lexicon. In the following issue of the Bulletin C.T. Fritsch underlines the desirability of having an up-to-date LXX lexicon (p. 5). Whilst the Executive Committee of the IOSCS was considering a working document, prepared by S.P. Brock and S. Jellicoe, on the LXX lexicon project, *BIOSCS* 4 (1971) carries a resumé of a paper read by W. Eisenbeis at an IOSCS meeting in the preceding year, entitled "Toward a lexicon and grammar of the Septuagint" (pp. 7f.). On the basis of his experiment on about two fifths of the book of Genesis, he outlines possible ways for carrying on the project. It should be noted, however, that his experiment consisted mainly in writing card indexes, or "slipping," but not defining senses and describing usages of actual LXX Greek words: for a more detailed appraisal of the Eisenbeis experiment, see R.A. Kraft, "The Eisenbeis experiment and proposals," in R.A. Kraft (ed.), *Septuagint Lexicography*, SBLSCS 1, 1972, pp. 25-29. Eisenbeis followed this with another paper presented at the IOSCS meeting in Uppsala in 1971 attended also by this editor: see a resumé of the paper in *BIOSCS* 5 (1972) 6. Following a LXX lexicon symposium organised by the IOSCS, held on 5 September 1972 in Los Angeles and based on the above-mentioned volume edited by R.A. Kraft,

vii

the IOSCS appointed in 1973 (?) Emanuel Tov as Editor designate of the LXX lexicon project to be assisted by an international team of scholars: Cross, Goshen-Gottstein, Hanhart and Wevers (chair). This team successfully obtained a one-year (1978-79) feasibility study grant from the National Endowment for the Humanities. Kraft, by way of progress report, gives an account of how the project had reached the stage where final reports were being written for submission to the NEH with an application for continued support of the project: see *BIOSCS* 12 (1979) 14-16. Between the lines of the report one can perceive new directions the project had begun to take, namely production of tools necessary for ultimate compilation of a LXX lexicon. In "Computer Assisted Tools for Septuagint Studies" in *BIOSCS* 14 (1981), jointly authored by Kraft and Tov, one is given a fuller picture of this new development. They state: "In the long run, the project aims at creating a comprehensive and flexible computer 'data bank'"(p. 29). They go on to say: "Once the bank is available ... the various scholarly projects (lexicographical, grammatical, textcritical, etc.) can proceed accordingly" (p. 32).

Whilst precisely what is meant by "accordingly" in the above quote is not immediately apparent, we have maintained all along that there is considerable mileage to be made from "lexicographical studies" assisted by such an obviously useful databank to actual writing of lexicon entries. Accordingly Dr J. Lee of Sydney University and I myself had been working for some time on a pilot project aimed at producing a fully fledged lexicon of the Minor Prophets in the Septuagint version in 1987 when a colloquium was organised in Melbourne with a view to exploring a range of problems and possibilities associated with Septuagint lexicography. More information on the background of this Australian project had been presented

Introduction

in a paper read by the present editor at the sixth IOSCS congress in Jerusalem in 1986: T. Muraoka, "Towards a Septuagint lexicon," in C.E. Cox (ed.), *VI Congress of the International Organization for Septuagint and Cognate Studies: Jerusalem 1986* [SBLSCS 23] (Atlanta, 1987), pp. 255-76.

The colloquium took place on 17 August 1987 at the University of Melbourne. The participants were G. Fox (Brisbane), R.G. Jenkins (Melbourne), J.A.L. Lee (Sydney), T. Muraoka (Melbourne), S.P. Swinn (Sydney), and E. Tov (Jerusalem). A number of other people were also present, though they did not present a paper. All the above-named participants had written an entry or entries of LXX words of their choice and those entries had been circulated among the participants in advance. The colloquium was devoted to a brief oral presentation of the results followed by a discussion of general and specific problems arising from the actual experiment with writing lexicon entries. We believe that it succeeded in bringing out in full relief some of the general and methodological issues of fundamental importance to be grappled with by LXX lexicographers.

One crucial and difficult issue which has been touched upon by almost all the participants was that of the relationship between the Hebrew and the Greek, "Greek words and Hebrew meanings," as aptly put in the title of Tov's paper. The question arises of course because the LXX is for the most part a work of translation. Leaving aside the question of the alleged Semitic sources of parts of the New Testament, a NT lexicographer ought to strive to determine what was intended by NT writers. But what is a lexicon of a translated document? It is sometimes said that what matters is the translator's intention. But what is the translator's intention and how can one discover it?

If he hits a difficult passage and renders it by using well-known Greek words, but the resultant translation as a whole does not make much sense, or he resorts to mechanical translaton by using stereotypic translation equivalents, what would one say his intention was? And when does a given translation equivalent begin to become stereotypic? In a brief article published in *Journal of Theological Studies* NS 35 (1984) 441-48 as a critique of a lexical study by J.W. Olley of the vocabulary for 'righteousness' in the LXX Isaiah, the present editor indicated his view that in the main the LXX ought to be read from within, that is to say, without reference to the Hebrew text. Of course this does not mean that the Greek meaning is always clear and indisputable. What it means is that one ought to let the Greek speak for itself. By comparing the present editor's lexical analysis of δικαίωμα in the LXX as presented in his Jerusalem paper referred to above (pp. 259f.) and that by Tov in his paper included in this volume (pp. 71-82) the reader will note an intriguing development in the latter's perception on this issue. See also his discussion of ἐπιφανής towards the end of the entry. As the organiser of the colloquium it was gratifying to reflect that the actual involvement in the writing of articles may have brought about this change on Tov's part, so much so that the present editor was said to be heeding the Hebrew too much.

Lee, in his paper "συνίστημι: a sample lexical entry," deals with a number of basic problems by closely analysing the usage of this compound verb with a wide spread of senses. He stresses that the task of a lexicographer compiling a bilingual dictionary is to define senses rather than list translation equivalents. Lee also attempts to trace ideational or semantic links between the various senses proposed for this Greek word on the ground

Introduction

that such a process can help sharpen the edge of definitions. His position regarding the relationship between the source language and the target language is summed up as: "the Hebrew is included only if the user of the lexicon needs it in order to appreciate the translator's intention" (p. 4). Then the author proceeds to a close examination of five particular senses of the verb which seem to give rise to a special difficulty or point of interest. A sample entry is included.

The first issue dealt with in the present editor's contribution, "Septuagintal lexicography: some general issues," is function words such as prepositions, conjunctions, pronouns. Their extremely high frequency, among other things, makes them the nightmare of a lexicographer. It may be genuinely asked whether they have "senses" in the way substantives, verbs, and the like can be said to have senses. A LXX lexicogapher has to cope with a practical difficulty as well in that a concordance, otherwise excellent, such as Hatch and Redpath's, does not provide the necessary information for most words of this category: it is either content with "passim" or merely lists the references without quoting the text. There is no doubt however that these words possess vital communicative value. The second issue raised in the paper is the basic task a lexicographer is required to perform. This is said to be definition of senses and description of usages, which latter includes aspects of orthography, morphology, syntax, idioms, collocations, synonyms, and antonyms. The third issue discussed is that of semantic field. Though we believe in the advantages of the alphabetical arrangement of entries, the importance of the structuralist approach to the vocabulary of a language must not be lost sight of. Vocabulary items semantically or ideationally related somehow need to be looked at in their mutual relationship.

Fourthly, whilst we do not subscribe to the "Jewish Greek" hypothesis, the presence of unique Septuagintal usage is in no doubt. Whether such usage developed under Semitic influence or not is a separate issue. One should not preclude the possibility that the LXX may attest to some unique development even independent of the Semitic original or background. The fifth and last section examines a few concrete examples to illustrate what kinds of difficulty may be encountered by a lexicographer approaching the LXX basically as a Greek document. The discussion of each of these five issues is accompanied by sample entries pertaining to the Minor Prophets.

Swinn's contribution entitled "Ἀγαπᾶν in the Septuagint" tackles the theologically charged and significant word ἀγαπᾶν and its derivatives vis-à-vis their kindreds, notably φιλεῖν. The centrality of the concept of love in the New Testament has produced a considerable amount of lexical work on ἀγαπᾶν, mostly stressing the alleged uniqueness of its usage in the Greek Bible as against its usage in the secular Greek. Swinn concurs with Joly, who had demonstrated that the shift from φιλεῖν to ἀγαπᾶν was on the way well before the appearance of the LXX, and thus the preponderance of the latter in Biblical Greek is an accurate reflection of this gradual linguistic evolution that had been taking place in the language, and was not motivated by any specially Hebraic/Christian theology. By analysing the usage of ἀγαπᾶν in the LXX Swinn attempts to show that the 'love' terminology of the LXX (and hence also of the NT) reflects the actual usage of the time and can be located on the plane of development from Classical to Modern Greek. His examination is confined to the Pentateuch, Isaiah and Proverbs. Like Joly, Swinn also adopts a structuralist approach by considering ἀγαπᾶν in relation to not only its

Introduction xiii

etymological derivatives such as ἀγαπητός, ἀγάπησις, but also synonyms φιλεῖν, ἐρᾶν, στέργειν and their derivatives, and the antonym μισεῖν.

In his pages, Tov's principal concern is with the question of semantic Semitism in the LXX Greek vocabulary and the practical problem of how to record Hebraistic usages in a lexicon. To illustrate some of the problems involved he chose to examine δικαίωμα, ὁμολογέω group, ἐπιφανής, and ὀρθρίζω. In the case of δικαίωμα, Tov isolates the senses 4) *decree, ordinance, regulation*, 5) *custom, manner*, and 6) *rightful due* as unique to the LXX. He further believes that the last two reflect the meaning of the Hebrew מִשְׁפָּט. Thus his entry reads, in part, as follows: 5. = מִשְׁפָּט *custom**(?), *manner**(?). As regards the ὁμολογέω group, the author argues that the sense "to give thanks," which appears to be attested in some places in the LXX and documents under its influence is problematic, and he suspects the influence of Heb. הוֹדָה. The case of ἐπιφανής is slightly different. None of the senses established by Tov is said to be unique to the LXX, but its assignation is made by reference to the Hebrew text; the author attempts to demonstrate that in some places the LXX attests to false etymology whereby נוֹרָא is derived from ראה when it should have been derived from ירא. The concluding section of Tov's study looks at what appears to be a Hebraistic adverbial use of the verb in the sense *early, earnestly* under the apparent influence of חָשַׁם. Tov's current position regarding the question of Semitism in relation to LXX lexicography is summed up thus: "... as long as possible we record the words of the LXX as if that text were a regular Greek text, explaining the words – conjecturally – in the way which a Greek reader would have taken them. After all, that is the task of the lexicographer of any text. Only when this procedure would lead to unrealistic results, when no feasible meaning can be derived from the Greek context, our knowledge about the translators' intentions is invoked" (p. 99).

It remains for the editor to express his gratitude to all the participants in the colloquium for their stimulating contributions, to Dr Cox for readily agreeing to include the present volume in the series Septuagint and Cognate Studies under his editorship, Dr Ford of Scholars Press for some valuable technical advice, and to the Department of Classical and Near Eastern Studies of my university for a grant towards covering some editorial cost. It is sincerely hoped that the colloquium marks a step closer to the actual production of a LXX lexicon, and that this volume stimulates further discussion on aspects of the complexity of LXX lexicography.

Takamitsu Muraoka
Dept. of Classical and Near Eastern Studies,
University of Melbourne, Parkville,
Victoria 3052, AUSTRALIA.

22nd May, 1989.

ABBREVIATIONS

AJBI	Annual of the Japanese Biblical Institute.
BAGD	W. Bauer, W.F. Arndt, F.W. Gingrich, and W. Danker, *A Greek-English Lexicon of the New Testament and Other Early Christian Literature*, Chicago ²1979.
BDB	F. Brown, S.R. Driver, and C.A. Briggs, *A Hebrew and English Lexicon of the Old Testament*, Oxford 1907.
BDF	F. Blass, A. Debrunner and R.W. Funk, *A Greek Grammar of the New Testament and Other Early Christian Literature*, Chicago 1961.
BHS	K. Elliger and W. Rudolph (eds), *Biblia Hebraica Stuttgartensia*, Stuttgart 1967-77.
Brenton	L.C.L. Brenton, *The Septuagint with Apocrypha: Greek and English*, London 1851.
Cyr.	*Sancti patris nostri Cyrilli Alexandrini in XII prophetas*, 2 vols., ed. Ph.E. Pusey (Oxford, 1868).
SBLSCS	*Journal of Biblical Literature*: Septuagint and Cognate Studies, currently edited by C.E. Cox.
KB	L. Koehler and W. Baumgartner, *Lexicon in veteris testamenti libros*, Leiden 1958.
Kittel	ThDNT (see below).
LSJ	H.G. Liddell, R. Scott and H.S. Jones, *A Greek-English Lexicon*, Oxford ⁹1940.
Mayser	E. Mayser, *Grammatik der griechischen Papyri aus der Ptolemäerzeit*, Berlin 1906-70.
MM	J.H. Moulton and G. Milligan, *The Vocabulary of the Greek Testament*, London 1930.
MT	Massoretic text, i.e. received Hebrew text
Preisigke	Preisigke-Kiessling (see below).
Preisigke-Kiessling	F. Preisigke and E. Kiessling, *Wörterbuch der griechischen Papyrusurkunden*

	etc., Berlin / Amsterdam 1925-71.
Schleusner	J.F. Schleusner, *Novus thesaurus philologico-criticus sive lexicon in LXX* etc., Leipzig 1820.
Th	H.St J. Thackeray, *A Grammar of the Old Testament in Greek*, Cambridge 1909.
ThDNT	G. Kittel (ed.) as translated by G.W. Bromiley, *Theological Dictionary of the New Testament*, 10 vols., Grand Rapids 1964-76.
Th Sp.	H.N. Sprenger, *Theodori Mopsuesteni commentarius in XII prophetas*, Wiesbaden 1977.
ThWB	*ThDNT* (see above).

συνίστημι: A SAMPLE LEXICAL ENTRY

John A.L. Lee

The word I have chosen is unexciting in thought-content, but provides a good illustration of the ordinary problems of lexical analysis. Like most compounds of verb and preposition, it has a wide spread of senses and so brings to notice many of the common difficulties of definition and classification. While much of the analysis is fairly routine, it does offer some challenges. In this paper the full lexical entry will be discussed briefly, and then we shall focus on some problematic senses that merit detailed discussion.

First of all some brief remarks on my general approach to the writing of a lexical entry. I see myself as being firmly in the tradition or 'school' of the *Oxford English Dictionary* and *Oxford Latin Dictionary*. At the heart of this approach is the framing of definitions. These form compartments which cover exactly the examples put into them. To put it another way: each definition describes as precisely as possible the area of meaning one intends to delimit, and every effort is made to avoid ambiguity. This approach is very different from what we find for example in LSJ. Its authors work rather from translation equivalents, i.e. possible translations in context. This is readily seen to be an unsatisfactory method. It is too loose a way of describing meanings, leading to confusion and error. This is not to say LSJ is not a valuable resource, but in the production of new dictionaries it is a

1

bad example to follow.

In my sample entry definitions will be distinguished typographically from possible translations (see below). Let us turn now to συνίστημι and what is involved in writing an entry for it. The first step is to assemble the LXX occurrences. For this we rely, as things stand at present, on the concordance of Hatch-Redpath. The occurrences are then checked in the Greek text (Göttingen edition where possible, otherwise Rahlfs), the corresponding Hebrew is examined, and a provisional meaning in each place is assigned. For the purpose of the present exercise I have taken the 25 examples between Genesis and 1 Maccabees as sufficient, and omitted some 18 in the 'literary and Atticistic' 2, 3 Maccabees. (Also omitted are: 1Ki 17.26 in verses described by Rahlfs as absent from G, Je 5.27 where συνίστημι is varia lectio, and examples in Da Th).

Having gathered our examples, how do we proceed? What have we to help us decide on definitions and classify? Our main resource is LSJ, which gives more or less all the lexical information so far assembled. We will also consult BAGD and Preisigke-Kiessling, and Schleusner is worth a glance. But even with these reference works, we need to be aware that the postclassical documentary and literary evidence is not properly under control. There is as yet no systematic collection, let alone lexical analysis, of the vast mass of material found in inscriptions, papyri, and literary texts from III BC to VI AD.

So we depend heavily on LSJ, and use its information gratefully, but with caution. In particular, it is a general rule that LSJ's analysis of meanings cannot be taken as a basis. We must start again and write our own definitions and work out our own classification.

συνίστημι

συνίστημι

A. Trans.

I.1. *introduce, commend* τινά τινι: συνέστησεν αὐτὸν πᾶσιν τοῖς φίλοις αὐτοῦ 1Ma 12.43; pass. διὰ τὰς ἐκ παιδείας δωρεὰς συσταθέντες, 'recommended by the gifts of training' Wi 7.14.

2. *place* (a person, τινα) *in the care or under the control of* (someone, τινι): συνέστησεν ὁ ἀρχιδεσμώτης τῷ Ἰωσὴφ αὐτούς, 'the chief jailer assigned them to Joseph's care' Ge 40.4.

3. mid. *combine*: συνεστήσαντο δύναμιν, 'they combined (their) power,' 'they joined forces' 1Ma 2.44.

II.1. act. and mid. *construct, form, arrange*: ὁ θεὸς εὖ συνέστησεν αὐτῆς [= σοφίας] τὴν ὁδόν Jb 28.23; ἀπὸ παγίδος ἧς συνεστήσαντό μοι, 'from the snare which they have set against me' Ps 140.9; συνεστήσαντο πόλιν κατοικεσίας 106.36.

2. act. and mid. *bring about, cause to occur*: ταραχὰς Pr 6.14; δόλον 26.26; συνίστασθαι πόλεμον πρός τινα, 'make war against' 1Es 1.27, Da LXX 7.21, 1Ma 1.2,18, 2.32, 3.3; πολιορκίας συνιστάμενοι 1Es 2.17.

3. mid. *hold, celebrate* (a festival): συστήσασθε ἑορτήν Ps 117.27.

III. *appoint* τινα to a position: ἐπέθηκεν τὰς χεῖρας αὐτοῦ ἐπ' αὐτὸν [= Ἰησοῦν] καὶ συνέστησεν αὐτόν Nu 27.23; συνέστησεν αὐτοῖς Μωυσῆς Ἐλεαζὰρ τὸν ἱερέα καὶ Ἰησοῦν υἱὸν Ναυὴ καὶ ... 32.28.

B. Intrans.

I.1. *accumulate, stand in a body*: πᾶν συνεστηκὸς ὕδωρ αὐτῶν Ex 7.19.

2. *band together* ἐπί τινα, with the notion of conspiracy: συνέστη ὁ λαὸς ἐπὶ Ἀαρών Ex 32.1, Nu 16.3.

3. *be blocked, congeal*: ἢ συνέστηκεν τὸ σῶμα αὐτοῦ

διὰ τῆς ῥύσεως, 'or (when) his body [ref. penis] is closed up because of the discharge' Le 15.3bis.
II. take shape, appear, stand: ἐν τῷ συστῆναι τὸν ἁμαρτωλὸν ἐναντίον μου Ps 38.2.

This specimen entry is of course the result of a lengthy process. We do not need to go through this in detail here. I simply give a general indication of the thinking behind the analysis adopted.

The division into transitive and intransitive is natural, and presents no problems in the case of this verb. Wi 7.14 (A.I.1) seems clearly to be a passive of a transitive use.

In A.I are grouped developments from the primary notion of placing together, causing persons or things to come together. Senses 1. and 2. refer to bringing persons together in particular relationships; 3. is close to the primary sense but somewhat developed.

A.II represents a different line of development, from the primary notion of assembling parts to form a whole. Sense 1. is fairly concrete, 2. more abstract, and 3. a further step developed out of 2.

A.III is an unexpected development. It is semantically not easy to trace from the primary sense(s). We shall consider it in more detail later.

Throughout A. I found no reason to separate middle forms from active. There is, as far as I can see, no discernible difference in lexical meaning.

Under B.I we have senses derived from the notion of standing together or standing combined. B.II, if correctly recognized, is a separate line. It is the intransitive corresponding to the transitive sense A.II.2. We shall need to consider this sense more closely also.

συνίστημι

At this point it may be asked what has become of the Hebrew in my entry. As you can see, it does not appear at all. Why is this, and under what circumstances would the Hebrew original be mentioned? The answer involves large questions of principle which we cannot go into in depth now. My answer in brief is as follows.

It is not to be doubted that the Hebrew original is highly relevant to the LXX lexicographer's task. What we have to decide, however, is the place it should have in the end result of the process, the lexical entry. Ultimately it is a question of what the LXX lexicon is aiming to do. The answer to this, in my view, is that it aims to display the meaning or meanings of the Greek word as arrived at by the editor after weighing all the available indications. The original Hebrew is one of these indications, but only alongside others (context, current uses, translator's habits, and so on). The aim of the lexicon is not to provide a register of correspondences between the LXX and its original. This is the province of some other work.

It follows, I believe, that the original Hebrew should be included in a lexical entry only if it is in some way involved in understanding the meaning of the Greek. Or we might put it this way: the Hebrew is included only if the user of the lexicon needs it in order to appreciate the translator's intention. This can happen in a number of ways, as for example where there is stereotyped rendering, or etymologizing, or where the Greek mirrors a Hebrew idiom strange to Greek.

My view on this matter is still developing and remains open to modification in the light of experience. It is in fact very difficult to lay down fixed rules in advance.

Everything depends on what is encountered in practice, and every word seems to present its own problems. At any rate, in my attempt at writing an entry for συνίστημι, although of course the Hebrew was taken into account, it did not seem to me to require mention anywhere.

An equally important matter is the question of the inclusion of parallels from outside the LXX. As you can see, I have not undertaken to include any. But ideally I think they should be included. Some indication of the Greek evidence outside the LXX is needed, I believe, for two purposes: (a) to support the senses recognized, and (b) to show the extent to which LXX usage conforms to or departs from attested Greek usage.

Let us turn now to a closer examination of some of the senses recognized in the above entry. I have selected five in which a special difficulty or point of interest arises. The data are tabulated first in each case, then discussion follows.

  A.I.2. *place* (a person, τινα) *in the care or under the control of* (someone, τινι): Ge 40.4

  καὶ συνέστησεν ὁ ἀρχιδεσμώτης τῷ Ἰωσὴφ αὐτούς, καὶ παρέστη αὐτοῖς· ἦσαν δὲ ἡμέρας ἐν τῇ φυλακῇ.
  וַיִּפְקֹד שַׂר הַטַּבָּחִים אֶת־יוֹסֵף אִתָּם וַיְשָׁרֶת אֹתָם וַיִּהְיוּ יָמִים בְּמִשְׁמָר:
  'place in the charge of'(LSJ s.v. A.IV.1.d.)
  '*committebat* princeps custodiae Iosepho illos' (Schleusner)
  P.Oxy. 724.2 (155 AD) συνέστησά σοι Χαιράμμωνα δοῦλον πρὸς μάθησιν σημείων ὧν ἐπίσταται ὁ υἱός σου
  *P.Cair.Zen.*600.15 (iii BC) [The writer refers Zenon to Eutychos for confirmation of the statement that he received only two mattocks] τούτωι [Eutychos] γὰρ συνεσ-

συνίστημι 7

τήσαμεν Αἴθωνα τὸν Μ[ ]ρίμου παῖδα, ὃς ἀπήνεγκεν ἡμῖν
τὰς β δικέλλας.
PSI 589.14 (iii BC) προσαξιῶ δέ σε καὶ εἰς τὸν λοιπὸν
χρόνον, εἰ καί σοι δοκεῖ, συστησόμ με Σώσωι, ὅπως ἂν
παρ' ἐκείνου λαμβάνωμεν [sc. ὀψώνιον] καὶ μή σε
ἐνοχλῶμεν.
Pl.*Theages* 122a [Demodocus has been speaking of his
son's wish to be taught by a sophist] νῦν οὖν ἥκω ἐπ'
αὐτὰ ταῦτα, ἵνα τῳ τούτων τῶν σοφιστῶν δοκούντων εἶναι
συστήσω τουτονί.

The meaning of συνίστημι here in Genesis is not at
once obvious. It would be *possible* to take it in the well-
established senses of 'recommend,' 'introduce,' even perhaps in the sense of 'place together with.' But none of
these seems to be quite right, and a better alternative
does not immediately suggest itself.
We must consider the Hebrew next. It says (very
literally): 'the captain of the guard appointed Joseph
with them and he served them.' That is, as I understand
it, the captain of the guard assigned Joseph to Pharaoh's
chief butler and chief baker as a servant.
The cast of the Greek is rather different. For a start
παρέστη is not really 'he served.' It has a vaguer sense
more like 'he was on hand,' or 'he was at their disposal.'
Joseph's position as a servant is covered over or made
more indistinct by this rendering. We recall that in the
preceding narrative Joseph has so found favour with the
prison governor as to be placed in charge of the running
of the prison (39.21-3). Then in the first clause of the
sentence the syntax has been slightly rearranged so that
we have 'them' as object instead of 'Joseph' (with אֹתָם
taken as אִתָּם ?). Thus we are led towards a meaning
something like 'he assigned them to Joseph.'

It is clear that LSJ have hit the mark. (A similar meaning is given by F.C. Conybeare and St G. Stock in their *Selections from the Septuagint* [Boston, 1905], and cf. already Schleusner.) LSJ add a parallel in *POxy.* 724, which provides some support, and further delving into the papyrological evidence turn up the two III BC examples given above. Moreover the occurrence in Plato's *Theages*, classified by LSJ under **IV.1.a.**, seems to me a clear instance of the same use. There the speaker clearly intends not simply to introduce his son to a sophist, but to place him as a pupil under one of them. These examples, then, provide good evidence for the currency of this use and enable us to appreciate the LXX properly. My definition is framed in the light of these four.

A.II.3.mid. *hold, celebrate* (a festival): Ps 117.27
θεὸς κύριος καὶ ἐπέφανεν ἡμῖν·
συστήσασθε ἑορτὴν ἐν τοῖς πυκάζουσιν
ἕως τῶν κεράτων τοῦ θυσιαστηρίου.
'celebrate the feast with *thick branches, binding the victims* even to the horns of the altar.
*Possibly, the multitude, *q.d.* coetu frequenti.'
(Brenton) 'Solemnise a festival with thick boughs, even to the horns of the altar'(Thomson-Muses)([1])
...' πυκάζουσιν (sc. κλάδοις) ... sistite vel figite festum *obumbrantibus ramis* usque ad cornua altaris, h.e. si verba per hypallagen quandam accipiamus: figite in festo obumbrantes ramos usque ad cornua altaris' (Schleusner)
אֵל יְהוָה וַיָּאֶר לָנוּ אִסְרוּ־חַג בַּעֲבֹתִים עַד־קַרְנוֹת הַמִּזְבֵּחַ:
'bind the festal victim with cords' (BDB: 'prob.')
'bind the festal procession with branches, up to the

([1]) A. Thomson, *The Septuagint Bible*, revised by C.A. Muses, Indian Hills, ²1960.

συνίστημι   9

horns of the altar!' (RSV)
'he has given light to us, the ordered line of pilgrims by the horns of the altar' (NEB)

This is a difficult case, and some guesswork is involved in assigning a meaning. While some sense can be made of συστήσασθε ἑορτήν on its own, the Greek context as a whole is obscure, and the original Hebrew no less so. The ground is therefore not very firm, but let us see if we can find our way to a reasonable conclusion.

The focus of difficulty in the Greek sentence is πυκάζουσιν. From LSJ we learn that πυκάζω is attested since Homer, is predominantly poetic, has some such meaning as 'cover thickly,' and is only *transitive* in the active as far as LSJ's evidence goes. In our present example, however, only an *intransitive* sense is workable, i.e. 'grow thickly,' 'spread thickly.' Since the context requires it, an intransitive use would have to be accepted even without support, but I find that out of the three other examples of the verb in the LXX two are in fact intransitive, viz. Jb 15.32 ὁ ῥάδαμνος αὐτοῦ οὐ μὴ πυκάσῃ, 'his branch will not grow thickly,' Ho 14.9 ἐγὼ ὡς ἄρκευθος πυκάζουσα, ἐξ ἐμοῦ ὁ καρπός σου εὕρηται, 'I am like a juniper growing thickly...'

The phrase ἐν τοῖς πυκάζουσιν, then, evidently means 'with or in the things that spread or grow thickly.' The reference is not *necessarily* to plant life (cf. Brenton's note), but this seems the best guess. It fits in with the way the word is used in the Job and Hosea examples, and also with one of the possible meanings of עבתים, i.e. 'branches' or 'thick foliage.'

As for ἑορτήν, I can see no possibility of taking this in anything but its established sense of 'festival.'

We must now try to make up our minds about συστήσασθε. The only possibilities seem to be 'institute' and 'celebrate.' I have opted for the latter, for no better reason than that it seems to me to fit the context best. As far as semantic development goes, there is no problem: both of these can be readily derived from existing senses, especially A.II.2. in my analysis. What about parallels? LSJ recognize neither of these senses, but under A.III.3. an example of συνίστασθαι ἑορτήν is cited from Apollod. 3.14.6, i.e. Apollodorus Mythographus, *Bibliotheca* (i AD[?]). The meaning there turns out to be, very probably, 'institute,' 'establish': Ἐριχθόνιος ... τῶν Παναθηναίων τὴν ἑορτὴν συνεστήσατο. Though this would support the sense I have rejected, I do not consider it decisive.

My translation, then, is: 'celebrate a festival with the thick-spreading vegetation up to the horns of the altar.'

As to the Hebrew original, I am not competent to discuss its problems in detail, but I believe I can understand how the Greek rendering was arrived at, and would submit that the LXX presents a reasonable interpretation of the Hebrew text.

אסרו is of course literally 'bind.' Its common equivalent is δέω, found some 26 times, including once in Psalms (149.8). συνίστημι is used as a rendering only in our present example, and this seems to me to be a rather skilful solution to the problem of אסר in an unprecedented combination, i.e. with חג, 'festival,' as object. It reproduces in a sort of a way the primary meaning of the Hebrew word (bind = put together), but at the same time allows a more developed, idiomatic sense that gives meaning to the combination.

One is tempted to go further and say that the LXX translators have understood the Hebrew rightly. We have

συνίστημι   11

after all the expression אסר המלחמה, generally understood
as 'begin the battle' (BDB, KB) so why not אסר חג with the
meaning 'hold a festival'? Both uses could be derived from
some such shared notion as 'set in train' or 'engage in.'
If this is right, no expedients are necessary in
understanding חג.([2])

[In the subsequent discussion Professor Tov was
inclined to doubt that we can be so definite about the
sense intended by the LXX translator: he may be attempting
only to represent the literal meaning of the Hebrew word,
without much concern for how it fits into the context.]

A.III. *appoint* τινα to a position: Nu 27.23, 32.28

²³ καὶ ἐπέθηκεν τὰς χεῖρας αὐτοῦ ἐπ' αὐτόν καὶ
συνέστησεν αὐτόν, καθάπερ συνέταξεν κύριος τῷ Μωυσῇ.
וַיִּסְמֹךְ אֶת־יָדָיו עָלָיו וַיְצַוֵּהוּ כַּאֲשֶׁר דִּבֶּר יהוה בְּיַד־מֹשֶׁה:
²⁸ καὶ συνέστησεν αὐτοῖς Μωυσῆς Ἐλεαζὰρ τὸν ἱερέα
καὶ Ἰησοῦν υἱὸν Ναυὴ καὶ τοὺς ἄρχοντας πατριῶν τῶν
φυλῶν Ἰσραήλ.
וַיְצַו לָהֶם מֹשֶׁה אֶת אֶלְעָזָר הַכֹּהֵן וְאֵת יְהוֹשֻׁעַ בִּן־נוּן וְאֶת־רָאשֵׁי
אֲבוֹת הַמַּטּוֹת לִבְנֵי יִשְׂרָאֵל:

There is no question that this is the right meaning.
The contexts require it and LSJ (**IV.1.e.**) supply adequate
parallels. The point of interest here is one of semantics
within Greek. How is the development of this sense to be
explained? It makes its appearance late on the scene, and
is not readily derivable from the primary meaning or from
any of the established senses. Nor is it a 'Hebraism.'

([2]) Cf. Ch.A. and E.G. Briggs, *Psalms*, ICC (Edinburgh,
1951-52), vol. 2, p. 409, for a similar argument; he
renders 'begin the feast.')

While none of this means that we should entertain serious doubts, it is nevertheless desirable, as a general principle, to trace the semantic development of all senses recognized, if it is at all possible.

There is, I think, an explanation available. If we look at the compound καθίστημι, we soon find that 'ordain,' 'appoint' is an old and well-attested sense (LSJ, s.v. A.II.2.a., e.g. with τύραννον as object). Likewise it turns out that the simplex ἵστημι is attested in this sense since Herodotus (LSJ, s.v. A.III.3., e.g. βασιλέα). What we probably have here, then, is an instance of a phenomenon that can be observed from time to time in Koine Greek, though I have not seen it systematically studied.([3]) It is one in which we find what might be termed 'semantic contamination' between different compounds of the one verb, or between compounds and simplex. It goes hand in hand with the well-known later Greek phenomenon of over-use of compounds, with preposition prefixes tending to lose their distinctive force. Thus it appears that συνίστημι acquired this new sense by transference from καθίστημι and ἵστημι.

B.I.3. *be blocked, congeal*: Le 15.3*bis*

Ἀνδρὶ ἀνδρί, ᾧ ἂν γένηται ῥύσις ἐκ τοῦ σώματος αὐτοῦ, ἡ ῥύσις αὐτοῦ ἀκάθαρτός ἐστιν. ³ καὶ οὗτος ὁ νόμος τῆς ἀκαθαρσίας αὐτοῦ· ῥέων γόνον ἐκ σώματος αὐτοῦ ἐκ τῆς ῥύσεως, ἢ συνέστηκεν τὸ σῶμα αὐτοῦ διὰ τῆς ῥύσεως. αὕτη ἡ ἀκαθαρσία αὐτοῦ ἐν αὐτῷ· πᾶσαι αἱ

([3]) For some other examples, see H. Anz, *Subsidia ad cognoscendum Graecorum sermonem vulgarem e Pentateuchi versione Alexandrina repetita* (Diss. Phi. Halenses XII.2) (Halle, 1894), p. 381, and my *A Lexical Study of the Septuagint Version of the Pentateuch* (Chico, 1983), p. 78.

συνίστημι 13

ἡμέραι ῥύσεως σώματος αὐτοῦ. ἡ συνέστηκεν τὸ σῶμα
αὐτοῦ διὰ τῆς ῥύσεως, ἀκαθαρσία αὐτοῦ ἐστιν. ⁴πᾶσα
κοίτη, ἐφ' ᾗ ἂν κοιμηθῇ ἐπ' αὐτῆς ὁ γονορρύης,
ἀκάθαρτος ἔσται, καὶ πᾶν σκεῦος, ἐφ' ὃ ἂν καθίσῃ ἐπ'
αὐτὸ ὁ γονορρυής, ἀκάθαρτον ἔσται.

³וְזֹאת תִּהְיֶה טֻמְאָתוֹ בְּזוֹבוֹ רָר בְּשָׂרוֹ אֶת־זוֹבוֹ אוֹ־הֶחְתִּים בְּשָׂרוֹ
מִזוֹבוֹ טֻמְאָתוֹ הִוא:
⁴כָּל־הַמִּשְׁכָּב אֲשֶׁר יִשְׁכַּב עָלָיו הַזָּב יִטְמָא וְכָל־הַכְּלִי אֲשֶׁר־יֵשֵׁב עָלָיו
יִטְמָא:

[In the paper as originally presented, my primary
concern here was with the reading of the text. Rahlfs'
text, with ἧς συνέστηκεν and ᾧ συνέστηκεν, creates great
difficulty in understanding συνέστηκεν. The solution,
clearly, is to read ἡ συνέστηκεν in both places, and this
reading had already been adopted by Wevers in the
Göttingen edition, which had not yet become available to
me.]

If we read ἡ *bis* as above we obtain a text which (a)
agrees with MT: ἡ συνέστηκεν is a fairly accurate
rendering of אוֹ־הֶחְתִּים ('or is stopped'); (b) makes good
sense: the syntax is a little disjointed, but the meaning
is clear; and (c) gives a known use of συνίστημι, or
something very close to it: cf. LSJ **A.V.** 'make solid'
etc., **B.V.** 'to be compact, solid, firm' etc., and note
also σύστασις B.II.3. 'density,' 'lump' etc.

B.II. *take shape, appear, stand*: Ps 38.2

²Εἶπα Φυλάξω τὰς ὁδούς μου τοῦ μὴ ἁμαρτάνειν ἐν
γλώσσῃ μου·
ἐθέμην τῷ στόματί μου φυλακὴν

ἐν τῷ συστῆναι τὸν ἁμαρτωλὸν ἐναντίον μου.
³ἐκωφώθην καὶ ἐταπεινώθην καὶ ἐσίγησα ἐξ ἀγαθῶν,
καὶ τὸ ἄλγημά μου ἀνεκαινίσθη.
²אָמַרְתִּי אֶשְׁמְרָה דְרָכַי מֵחֲטוֹא בִלְשׁוֹנִי
אֶשְׁמְרָה לְפִי מַחְסוֹם בְּעֹד רָשָׁע לְנֶגְדִּי:
'ἐν τῷ συστῆναι: ubi aut sensum expresserunt, aut pro
בעוד legerunt בעמד. Συστῆναι autem h.l. non est i.q.
simplex στῆναι, sed *conspirationis* et *coniurationis* no-
tionem adiunctam habet' (Schleusner).

It was difficult to make a decision here, and I am not
entirely happy with the definition finally arrived at. By
adding *stand* I have to some extent compromised; ideally it
would be better to choose between *stand* and *take shape,
appear*.
   At first sight it looks as if the translator saw, or
thought he saw, בעמד where MT has בעד, and intended
συστῆναι to mean simply 'stand,' without discernible
difference from στῆναι. This interpretation is reflected
in Brenton's rendering ('while the sinner stood in my
presence') and in the note in *BHS* (footnote ᶜ: 'LXX ἐν τῷ
συστῆναι, 1 בְּעֲמֹד,' though it is not made clear what
meaning the editors would assign to συστῆναι).
   But then doubts begin to surface. If the translator
intended no more than the meaning 'stand,' why not use
στῆναι? (This is the standard equivalent of עמד; συνίστημι
is found as a rendering only in 1Ki 17.26, with the
meaning 'stand together' [with].) Is the compound without
significance?
   Schleusner, as one can see, thought συστῆναι carried
the notion of conspiracy (cf. LSJ B.III.1., 'form a league
or union, band together,' and my B.I.2.). This is at-
tractive, but hard to fit into the context. We end up with
something like 'when the sinner banded together opposite

συνίστημι

me,' which seems very awkward.

I was inclined to see here a sense like LSJ's B.IV.1.c. and d. ('arise, take shape'; 'come into existence, exist'). This makes συστῆναι not exactly equivalent to στῆναι, though the effect in the context is nearly the same.

The question remains: what Hebrew was read by the translator? This is difficult to resolve, and I continue to vacillate. It is *possible* for the rendering to have arisen from the same text as MT (as Schleusner also suggested); on the other hand, that a part of ἵστημι is found corresponding to a form that could so easily be corrupted to or from בעמד seems to be more than just coincidence. At any rate, whatever the answer to this question, I have taken the step of assigning to συστῆναι a nuance not conveyed by στῆναι alone.

SEPTUAGINTAL LEXICOGRAPHY: SOME GENERAL ISSUES

Takamitsu Muraoka

1. **FUNCTION WORDS**

The vocabulary of a language is sometimes grouped into function words or empty words on the one hand, and full words on the other.(¹) The former division consists of categories such as prepositions, conjuctions, adverbs, pronouns, the article, etc. Though these constitute in any language a real minority of the total vocabulary, in terms of frequency in actual speech and written documents, they account for a most disproportionate amount of words. The very last sentence I have just written contains a total of 32 words, out of which as many as 15 are classifiable as function words. Thus function words are a nightmare of lexicographers. We also know that in any ancient text preserved in more than one manuscript these words usually provide a high percentage of variant readings. It is no doubt on the ground of this extremely high frequency that the LXX concordance compiled by Hatch and Redpath is usually content with giving only references without actually citing texts, and pronouns, conjunctions and the like being dismissed with "*passim.*"

(¹) For this classification of words, see H. Sweet, *A New English Grammar: Logical and Historical*, Part 1 (Oxford, 1891), § 58, and C.C. Fries, *American English Grammar: The Grammatical Structure of Present-Day American English with Especial Reference to Social Differences or Class Dialects* (New York, 1940), p. 109.

The problems presented by function words do not end with their high frequency. From the point of view of linguistic communication, they play a variety of highly important roles: many of them indicate logical relationships between words, phrases, clauses, and utterances. Their precise function is determined by the context to a greater degree than in the case of the other category of words, full words. Even taken on its own, and out of actual context, it is fairly easy to picture in one's mind the meaning of ἀνήρ, which would hardly be the case with the preposition, say, ἀνά or the particle δέ. The classification and description of senses and usage of function words is a very demanding task. Some may even doubt whether a preposition can have meanings or senses. However that may be, the complexity of the task facing a lexicographer is illustrated by the fact that the *Oxford English Dictionary* lists as many as 33 "senses" for the preposition *to*, excluding its use when prefixed to the infinitive.

Despite the enormity of the task in this particular area of lexicography, no lexicographer will have discharged his task creditably without paying due attention to this time-consuming but significant portion of the vocabulary of whatever language he is working with. Here one must follow in the footsteps of S.R. Driver, who was made responsible for "all pronouns, prepositions, adverbs, conjunctions, interjections, and other particles, together with some nouns whose principal use is adverbial."[2] We all know what a marvellous and valuable service he rendered for Hebrew and Biblical scholarship, although most Hebrew students are content with having learned that the preposition Lamed means "to," and do not bother to

---

[2] BDB, p. ix. W. Bauer's dictionary, abbreviated here as BAGD, also excels in this respect.

Some general issues   19

study a full description of its rich usage given by Driver
in over eight closely printed pages in two columns.
We present below our sample entries for ἕκαστος, ἕως,
ἤ, and μή.(³) Compare our entry for ἤ with that in
Schleusner.(⁴) To be fair to Schleusner, however, it must
be said that his presentation of data is determined by the
general philosophy underlying his lexicon, which is
basically translator-orientated, his basic concern being
what Hebrew word or words lies or lie behind a given LXX
word.

The reader will further note that in the description of
function words lexicography often borders on grammar.

ἕκαστος, η, ον.   pron.
each, separately and severally from the rest, 'on one's
own,' emphasising individuality or independence: ἀναπαύ-
σεται ἕκαστος ὑποκάτω ἀμπέλου αὐτοῦ 'each will take rest
under his own vine' Mi 4.4. There are a number of
patterns for grammatical agreement between the pronoun
on the one hand, and the verb and other associated
adjuncts on the other.
    a. the pron. in the sg. and the verb in the pl., but
the adjuncts in the sg.: πάντες οἱ λαοὶ πορεύσονται

(³) The dagger (†) at the end of the first line of a
given entry signifies that all the attestations of the
word in the corpus, the Minor Prophets, are mentioned in
the entry. The asterisk (*) signifies that the usage or
sense so marked is unique to the LXX in the present state
of our knowledge.
(⁴) J.F. Schleusner, *Novus Thesaurus Philologico-criticus
sive Lexicon in LXX* etc., Leipzig, 1820.

ἕκαστος τὴν ὁδὸν αὐτοῦ 'all the nations will go each its own way' Mi 4.5; ἕκαστος τὴν πλησίον αὐτοῦ ἐκθλίβουσιν 'each afflicting his own neighbour' ib. 7.2; ὑμεῖς διώκετε ἕκαστος εἰς τὸν οἶκον αὐτοῦ 'you run each into his own house' Hg 1.9; Jl 2.7 +. Cf. Za 10.1 (αὐτοῖς ... ἑκάστῳ).
b. the verb in the sg.: ἕκαστος ἀπὸ τοῦ ἀδελφοῦ αὐτοῦ οὐκ ἀφέξεται Jl 2.8 (MT: pl.).
c. the adjuncts also in the pl.: ἀνεβόων ἕκαστος πρὸς τὸν θεὸν αὐτῶν 'they called aloud each to his own god' Jn 1.5 (MT: sg.).
d. the adjuncts partly in the sg. and partly in the pl.: κακίαν ἕκαστος τοῦ ἀδελφοῦ αὐτοῦ μὴ μνησικακείτω ἐν ταῖς καρδίαις ὑμῶν 'do not remember each his own brother's injury in his heart' Za 7.10; ἐξαποστελῶ πάντας τοὺς ἀνθρώπους ἕκαστος ἐπὶ τὸν πλησίον αὐτοῦ 'I will send all the people each to his own neighbour' Za 8.10, sim. ib. 8.17.

The pronoun is often used in the form of ἕκαστος ...τὸν πλησίον (or ἀδελφὸν) αὐτοῦ (or in some other appropriate case): e.g. Za 3.10, Hg 2.22.

(3) a. שׁ־אִ [24], d. אִישׁ [1]; (-)[1]. Del. Am 1.11, v.l.(⁴ᵃ)

ἕως †

A. prep. w. gen. (exc. 7 below), *up to, as far as*, giving the end-point or limit of a movement, either local or temporal:

1. Ob 20(b), 20(-), Am 6.14(b), 8.12a(b), Mi 1.14(b: MT /ʻl/),15(b), 5.3(b), ἕ. ἄκρων τῆς γῆς 'to the far ends of the earth' ib. 5.4(b), μετὰ αὐτὸν οὐ προστεθήσεται ἕως ἐτῶν εἰς γενεὰς γενεῶν 'after it there will not be

---

(⁴ᵃ) The numbering of the Hebrew/Aramaic equivalents accords with those in Hatch and Redpath.

Some general issues   21

again for many generations of years to come' Jl 2.2(b);
ἔ. ψυχῆς Jn 2.6(b); ἔ. θανάτου, distressed 'to the point
of death' ib. 4.9(a); ἕως θανάτου ἐκδικηθήσεται Za 5.3;
ἔ. θεμελίου 'even to the foundation, thoroughly' Na
1.10(b); ἔ. τραχήλου Hb 3.13(b); Za 9.10(b), 14.5(e).
2. w. verbs of movement: ἥκω Mi 4.10(b), ἐξαποστέλλω Ob
7(b), εἰσέρχομαι Am 6.14(b), ἔρχομαι Mi 1.9(b) ter.
3. w. the two extreme points given: ἀπὸ βορρᾶ ἕως
ἀνατολῶν Am 8.12b(d); ἀπὸ τοῦ νῦν καὶ ἕως εἰς τὸν αἰῶνα
Mi 4.7(b); ib.6.5(b), 7.12(d); ἀπὸ μεγάλου αὐτῶν ἕως
μικροῦ αὐτῶν Jn 3.5(d); Za 14.10bis(c,b).
4. ἕως τίνος 'until when, how long?' Ho 8.5(b), Hb
1.2(b), 2.6(b), Za 1.12(b).
5. ἕως τοῦ + inf.: Ho 7.4(b), 10.12(b); with nuance of
result, Mi 7.9(a).
6. ἕως οὖ + aor.subj.: ἕως οὖ ἀφανισθῶσι καὶ ἐπιζητή-
σουσι (fut.!) 'in the end they will be annihilated and
start seeking ...' Ho 5.15(a), ἕως οὖ ἀπίδῃ ...'waiting
for the moment to see ...' Jn 4.5(a).
7. w. another prep.: ἕως εἰς μακράν Mi 4.3(b), ἕως εἰς
τὸν αἰῶνα Mi 4.7(b).
B. conj. w. subj. or fut., until or whilst: ἕως ἀγάγω
... καὶ ἥξει Mi 1.15 (b[MT:/ʽōd/]). See above under A.
7.

a. עַד אֲשֶׁר [4]; b. עַד [29]; c. לְ [1]; d. וְעַד [2]; e.
אֶל [1]; f. (-) [1].

ἤ   †

1. or: only the essential part(s) is (are) given after
ἤ: εἰ κλέπται εἰσῆλθον πρὸς σὲ ἢ λῃσταὶ νυκτός Ob 5(b);
Am 3.12(c), Za 11.12(h), Mi 6.7(-),8(d), Jl 1.2(f), Jn
4.11b(g), Hg 2.12(d)quater, Za 7.5(d)bis, Ma 2.13(d);
*b. introducing a disjunctive and complete interrogative

sentence, Ho 14.10(-), Mi 4.9(b), 6.3(d),3(-), Jl 3.4(f), Hb 3.8(b)bis, but with no choice or selection intended, introducing a sentence of synonymous import, 'or again', εἰ προσδέξεταί σε, ἤ (only in Arm and Eth with MT!) εἰ λήμψεται πρόσωπόν σου Ma 1.8(c), καὶ τίς ὑπομενεῖ ἡμέραν εἰσόδου αὐτοῦ; ἤ (καὶ A Eth Arm with MT!) τίς ὑποστήσεται ἐν τῇ ὀπτασίᾳ αὐτοῦ; ib.3.2(d), a usage distinct from what is discussed in BAGD, s.v. 1.d.β.

2. in comparison, than: καλῶς...τότε ἤ νῦν 'better then than now' Ho 2.7(a); an adjective or adverb understood, θέλω ... ἐπιγνῶσιν θεοῦ ἤ ὁλοκαυτώματα 'I prefer ... knowledge of God to a burnt-offering' Ho 6.6(a); καλὸν τὸ ἀποθανεῖν με ἤ ζῆν με Jn 4.3(a),8(a); with a quantifying expression, πλείους ἤ δώδεκα μυριάδες ἀνθρώπων 'more than twelve myriad people' Jn 4.11(a).

3. ἀλλ' ἤ, except: τί ἄλλο ἀλλ' ἤ σπέρμα ζητεῖ ὁ θεός; 'what else other than a seed does God seek?' Ma 2.15(-); in τί κύριος ἐκζητεῖ παρὰ σοῦ ἀλλ' ἤ τοῦ ποιεῖν κρίμα... 'what does the Lord require of you other than for you to practise justice ...?' Mi 6.8b(e), ἄλλο may be understood or a negative may be implied as in 1Clem. 13.4 ἐπὶ τίνα ἐπιβλέψω, ἀλλ' ἤ ἐπὶ τὸν πραῢν καὶ ἡσύχιον καὶ τρέμοντά μου τὰ λόγια;. See BDF, § 448.8. b. but, foll. a negative: "Not in great strength nor in power, ἀλλ' ἤ ἐν πνεύματί μου" Za 4.6.

See M.L. Margolis, "The particle ἤ in Old Testament Greek," AJSL 25 (1909) 257-75.

a. מִן [5]; b. אִם [3]; c. אִי [2]; d. ו [10]; e. אִם כִּי [1]; f. וְאִם [2]; g. לְ...בֵּין [1]; h. וְאִם לֹא [1]; (-) [4].

Schleusner: vol. 3, p. 15

*Η. quam, in comparatione. *םא. Iob. IV,12.
Legerunt יא. - *אל, non. Ies. X,15. Legerunt יא.
- ט praefixum. Psalm. CXVII,9. Ies. VII, 15. ubi
illud ή prorsus delendum esse videtur. Omittitur
interdum ante ή comparativus μᾶλλον aut similis,
e. c. Sirac. XLI,12. αὐτὸ (sc. fama bona) γὰρ
διαμένει, ή μεγάλοι θησαυροί. Cf. Munthe Obss.
in N.T. e Diodoro Siculo ad Matth. XVIII,9.

μή. negative particle. †
I. Usually placed immediately before a verb and thus
negativing the entire statement. The verb, if not inf.,
impv. or ptc., is invariably in the subj. mood (see BDF,
§ 426).
1. ὅπως μὴ λάβητε ἀδικίαν Ho 14.3(1); ἐὰν μὴ γνωρίσωσιν
ἑαυτούς Am 3.3(g),4(g),7(h), 5.6(m), Mi 3.8(i), 5.7(b),
Jl 2.17(n), Za 12.7(b),14.17(b),18(bbis),19(b), Ma
2.2(jbis). b. Once w. indic., but μή is part of a compound particle εἰ μή 'unless' (see BDF, § 428.3): εἰ μή
Γαλααδ ἐστιν Ho 12.11(k).
2. Indicating a prohibition or a negative wish: a. w. a
verb in the 2nd pers., μὴ ἐπίδῃς...μὴ ἐπιχαρῇς ... μὴ
μεγαλορρημονήσῃς Ob 12(ater), μὴ δῷς Jl 2.17(a);Jn
1.14²(a), Ma 2.15(a); b. w. a verb in the 1st pers.,
μὴ ἀπολώμεθα 'let us not perish' Jn 1.14¹(a); c. w. a
verb in the third pers., μὴ περάνῃ 'let him not finish'
Hb 2.5(b); d. + pres. impv., μὴ ἀγνόει ... μὴ εἰσπορεύεσθε ... μὴ ἀναβαίνετε ... μὴ ὀμνύετε Ho 4.15
(aquat); ib. 9.1(a), Am 5.5(a, bbis), 7.16(b), Mi
1.10(abis), 2.6(a), 7.5(abis), 8(a), Za 1.4(a),7.10
(abis), 8.17(abis); + aor. impv., μὴ γευσάσθωσαν 'let
them not taste' Jn 3.7(a); Ze 3.16(a).

3. τοῦ μή + inf. of purpose: τοῦ μὴ καλύπτειν 'in order (for her) not to cover' Ho 2.9(-); Am 6.10(b),14(c), Ze 3.6(e); "they made their ears heavy in order not to listen (τοῦ μὴ εἰσακούειν) and made their heart disobedient in order not to listen (τοῦ μὴ εἰσακούειν) to my law" Za 7.11f(cbis). b. after a verb of negative nuance such as verbs of withholding, preventing etc. (BDF,§ 400.4): ἀπώσομαί σε τοῦ μὴ (v.1.) ἱερατεύειν μοι 'I will reject you (and not allow you) to serve as a priest for me' Ho 4.6(c) (see AJBI 9 [1983] 35); "I will set up a defence for my house so that they may not pass through (τοῦ μὴ διαπορεύεσθαι)" Za 9.8(d). See Soisalon-Soininen, Die Infinitive in der Septuaginta, pp.75-80. c. after an adj.: καθαρὸς ὀφθαλμὸς τοῦ μὴ ὁρᾶν πονηρά 'an eye too pure to behold wicked things' Hb 1.13(c).

4. + ptc.: τοὺς μὴ ζητήσαντας ... τοὺς μὴ ἀντεχομένους Ze 1.6(bbis); Ma 3.5(b),18(b).

5. + subj., indicating a negative purpose, 'in order that ... not' (= ἵνα μή, ὅπως μή): μὴ ἔλθω καὶ πατάξω 'so that I may not come and strike, lest I should...' Ma 4.5(f).

II. Negating part of a sentence which gives a command: ἐκζητήσατε τὸ καλὸν καὶ μὴ τὸ πονηρόν 'Seek the good and not the evil' Am 5.14(a); sim. Jl 2.13(a).

III. Introducing a rhetorical question to which a negative answer is expected: μὴ σφάγια καὶ θυσίας προσηνέγκατέ μοι; 'Surely you have not offered me victims and sacrifices?' Am 5.25(d), μὴ βασιλεὺς οὐκ ἦν σοι; 'surely you had a king?' Mi 4.9(d); Am 2.11(d) (on the double negative, which expects an affirmative answer, see BAGD, s.v. C,1 end); ib. 6.10(d), Jl 3.4(d), Hb 3.8(d). Also Za 8.6(-). Perh. under the Heb. influence, the μή may be found in the middle of the question: οἱ προφῆται μὴ τὸν αἰῶνα ζήσονται; Za 1.5(d), sim. ib. 7.5(d).

(a) אֶל [27]   (b) לֹא [15]   (c) מִן [5]   (d) הֲ־ [9]   (e) מִבְּלִי [1]   (f) פֶּן [1]   (g) ἐὰν μή בִּלְתִּי [2]   (h) ἐὰν μή כִּי אִם [1]   (i) ἐὰν μή אוּלָם [1]   (j) ἐὰν μή אִם לֹא [2]   (k) μὴ εἰμι אַיִן [1]   (l) בַּל [1:Ho 14.3 k > b]   (m) ὅπως μή פֶּן [1]   (n) ὅπως μή לָמָה [1]   (o) וְלֹא [1]   (-) [2] Del. the foll. passages (v.l.): Am 9.10, Ze 1.12, 3.13, Ma 1.9(?), 3.8.

On οὐ μή, οὐδὲ μή, οὐδὲ οὐ μή, οὐκέτι μή, and οὐκέτι οὐ μή, see under οὐ.

2. DEFINITION OF SENSES, DESCRIPTION OF USAGES

Where one is dealing with bilingual or multilingual dictionaries, a number of different strategies are possible. Some dictionaries are not much different from glossaries customarily tacked at the end of an edition of an ancient text or chrestomathy, listing translation equivalents; as an example, one may mention a fairly widely used Langenscheidt's Biblical Hebrew dictionary. Others may go a little further by providing information on matters such as common collocations entered into by a given word, or prepositions with which a given word is prefixed, or information on author or authors who attest to a given sense or usage of the word optionally illustrated by citations.

We believe that a LXX lexicon ought to aim at providing the maximum information practicable on the usage of all LXX words. As one can see from our sample entries, this begins with morphological information. The general grammatical description of LXX Greek ought of course to be left to special grammars, but facts concerning individual words must be recorded in a lexicon.

The major part of any entry is of course a description of the senses and usage of the word concerned.

a. We prefer definition to mere listing of translation equivalents in English. In this we follow Glare's *Oxford Latin Dictionary*([5]) as against Lewis and Short's dictionary, though we do not adopt the former's format of presentation of data whereby a series of numbered definitions is followed by citations in small print. For example, see i,j,k in our entry for γινώσκω below.

γινώσκω: fut. γνώσομαι, pass. γνωσθήσομαι; aor. ἔγνων, 3pl. ἔγνωσαν, inf. γνῶναι; pf. ἔγνωκα. †

Under the primary sense of *to come to know*, a variety of nuances can be identified: a. *to come to know, learn, find out by observation or inquiry*: τὸν λογισμὸν κυρίου Mi 4.12 (// συνιέναι); "what she was going to face" Am 3.10; οὐκ ἔγνωσαν δεξιὰν αὐτῶν ἢ ἀριστερὰν αὐτῶν 'did not know their right hand nor their left hand' Jn 4.11; + ὅτι. Jn 1.10, 12 (ἔγνωκα = οἶδα); + διότι Za 2.9 (// ἐπιγινώσκειν 2.11).
b. *to have in the mind, to have learnt* (= οἶδα): τί ἐστι ταῦτα; Za 4.5; + ὅτι Jn 4.2.
c. *to be or become acquainted w., to gain close knowledge of*: + acc.pers., Ho 5.3; τὸν κύριον ib. 6.3b,

---

([5]) P.G.W. Glare (ed.), *Oxford Latin Dictionary* (Oxford, 1968-82).

cf. 6.3a (abs.); ὁ θεὸς, ἐγνώκαμέν σε ib.8.2; τὰ ἔθνη Za 7.14; pass., γνωσθῇ ἡ δικαιοσύνη τοῦ κυρίου Mi 6.5; + acc.rei, ἀσεβείας Am 5.12, τὴν δόξαν κυρίου Hb 2.14.

d. *to recognise, admit to acquaintance with:* ἄλων καὶ ληνὸς οὐκ ἔγνω αὐτούς 'the threshing-floor and winepress refused to recognise them' Ho 9.2.

e. *to experience:* κακά 'misfortune' Mi 4.9.

f. *to be or become aware:* "strangers devoured his resources without him becoming aware thereof" Ho 7.9a, sim. 7.9b.

g. *to recognise as one's own:* ἔγνω αὐτοὺς ὁ θεός Ho 11.12 (cf. Th. Sp. 62: οἰκειώσομαι), sim. Am 3.2.

h. *to identify:* οὐκ ἔγνω τὸν τόπον αὐτῆς Na 3.17.

i. *to acknowledge as true, important,* etc.: θεὸν πλὴν ἐμοῦ οὐ γνώσῃ 'you shall not recognise any other god than me' Ho 13.4; τὸ κρίμα 'to recognise the importance of justice' Mi 3.1.

j. *to take note of, not neglect one who is in some special need:* ἐν ἡμέρᾳ θλίψεως ... εὐλαβουμένους αὐτόν Na 1.7.

k. *to admit to the veracity of a proposition:* + ὅτι, Ho 2.8, 11.3; + διότι, Za 11.11.

Cf. γνωρίζω, γνῶσις, ἐπιγινώσκω, κατανοέω, οἶδα, and συνίημι. See also Bultmann in Kittel, 1.689-92, 696-701.

(4) ידע a. qal[28: incl. Ho 9.2 *r > d*; ib.11.12, word div.; Mi 4.9 MT *try'y*], *b.* ni.[1]. (-)[1: Hb 3.2]. Del. Jl 3.17, Za 2.11, 6.15, Ma 2.4, v.l.(v. s. ἐπι~); Ze 3.5, v.l.

Where a dictionary which merely gives translation equivalents may have a rather brief entry for κεφαλή, ours attempts to show a very rich and wide range of applications of the primary sense 'head.'

κεφαλή, ῆς. f. †
head, lit., of the sun beating down on one's head, Jn 4.8; 2.6, 4.6 *bis*; it may go bald, Am 8.10; where a head-dress (κίδαρις) is worn, Za 3.5 *bis*; a crown (στέφανος) is placed there, ib. 6.12; αἴρω ~ήν 'to raise one's head', of one who has been humiliated, ib. 1.21. Esp. as an object of physical violence and as a vulnerable spot: ἐκονδύλιζον ~ὰς πτωχῶν Am 2.7, διάκοψον εἰς ~ὰς πάντων, ib. 9.1, διέκοψας ~ὰς δυναστῶν, Hb 3.14, ἔβαλες εἰς ~ὰς ἀνόμων θάνατον 'you have sent death upon the heads of the unlawful' ib. 3.13; a place upon which a punitive action is brought down, ἀνταποδώσω τὸ ἀνταπόδομα ὑμῶν εἰς ~ὰς ὑμῶν Jl 3.7, sim. Ob 15.

(5) a. ראש [14]; (-) [1]. Del. Am 5.11 v.l.

Compare our entry of ἐξαποστέλλω with that of LSJ. Ours brings out a somewhat richer range of usage and nuances of the word, and this despite the fact that our corpus is very much narrower in scope.

ἐξαποστέλλω: 1aor. ἐξαπέστειλα; pf. ἐξαπέσταλκα.
1. to *dispatch, send out*: of envoy, + πρός + acc.pers., Hg 1.12, Za 2.11, 4.9; envoy understood, Am 7.10; πρὸ προσώπου σου τὸν Μωυσῆν καὶ Ααρων καὶ Μαριαμ as your leaders, Mi 6.4; εἰς place, Za 7.2; τὸν ἄγγελόν μου Ma 3.1; ἐξαποστελλόμενος 'envoy, emissary' Mi 1.14; δρέπανον 'sickle' Jl 3.13. b. of message, τοὺς λόγους ...ἐν χερσὶ τῶν προφητῶν Za 7.12; a commandment, πρὸς ὑμᾶς τὴν ἐντολὴν ταύτην Ma 2.4. c. of hostile, threatening object: πῦρ εἴς τινα, 'set fire to' Ho 8.14, Am 1.4,12; πῦρ ἐπὶ τὰ τείχη Am 1.7,10; πῦρ ἐπί τινα Am 2.2,5; εἰς ὑμᾶς θάνατον Am 4.10; λιμὸν ἐπὶ τὴν γῆν Am 8.11; ἡ δύναμίς μου ἡ μεγάλη 'my great army (of ravaging

Some general issues   29

insects) ... εἰς ὑμᾶς Jl 2.25; περιοχήν 'a besieging
army'(?; q.v.) εἰς τὰ ἔθνη Ob 1; πάντας τοὺς ἀνθρώπους
ἕκαστον ἐπι τὸν πλησίον αὐτοῦ 'set everybody on one
another' Za 8.10; ἐφ' ὑμᾶς τὴν καταράν Ma 2.2.
2. *to expel, drive out*: ἕως τῶν ὁρίων 'to the borders'
Ob 7.
3. *to divorce* (a wife), Ma 2.16.
4. *to release*: δεσμίους 'prisoners' Za 9.11.

   Cf. ἀποστέλλω and J.A.L. Lee, *A Lexical Study of the
Septuagint Version of the Pentateuch* (Chico, 1983), pp.
93f.

   (8) שׁלּח a. qal [12], b. pi.[15], d. hi.[1]. Del. f.
שׁלּוּחִים read ⸌šluḥîm⸍ or ⸌šlîḥîm⸍).

LSJ, s.v.

       ἐξαποστέλλω, fut. -στελῶ LXX 4Ki.8.12: pf. ἐξαπέ-
       σταλκα Attal.(v. infr.): --*dispatch* πρεσβυτάς Plb.
       3.11.1; στρατηγόν D.S.19.102; θεωρούς SIG629.8
       (Delph., ii B.C.); βιβλίον τινί Attal.ap.Hipparch.
       1.3.3; -- Pass., *to be dispatched*, Philipp.a.p.d.
       18.77, OGI90.20 (Rosetta, ii B.C.); ὑπό τινων Vit.
       Philonid.p.7C.; ἐξαπεσταλμένοι μάχεσθαι Aristeas
       13; also ἡμῶν ὁ λόγος -εστάλη Act.Ap.13.26.
       2. *send forth*, [δαίμων] -στέλλων ὕδατα καὶ ἀνέμους
       Sammelb.4324.16. 3. of prisoners, *send before a
       tribunal*, ἐ. τινὰ δέσμιον πρός τινας PTeb.22.18
       (ii B.C.), etc. --Pass., PTaur.I iii 13 (ii B.C.).
       II. *send away, dismiss*, e.g.: prisoner, Plb.4.
       84.3; ἐ. τινὰ κενόν *send away* empty-handed, Ev.
       Luc. 1.53; *divorce* a wife, LXX De.24.4; *expel*, ἐκ

τοῦ παραδείσου ib.Ge.3.23. **III.** *discharge* a projectile, Hero Bel.81.4(Pass.). **IV.** *destroy*, ὀχυρώματα ἐν πυρί LXX 4Ki.8.12. **V.** *emit, display*, φαντασίαν Procl.Hyp.5.72.

Provision of such information is important and useful for full appreciation of LXX Greek and the literature influenced by it, namely, NT, patristic Greek, Byzantine and Modern Greek. These aspects help us enter the cultural milieu and thought-world of the Hellenistic era, Hellenistic Judaism and Early Christian Church.

b. COLLOCATIONS

By long usage many words tend to form close association with certain other words, a phenomenon known as collocation.[6] Such collocations have the effect of defining nuances of the words' meanings. The entry given above for γινώσκω will illustrate the point. Thus what kinds of nouns the verb takes as its objects is of lexicographical interest and importance. Similarly the verb ἀγαπάω necessarily involves two parties. Leaving aside the non-animate entity as the object, it is important to classify the occurrences in our corpus of the verb according to whether the two parties are human or divine. The knowledge that when both are human, the subject is hardly ever female throws some interesting anthropological or sociological light on the nature of human love in the

---

[6] See M. Silva, *Biblical Words & their Meaning: An Introduction to Lexical Semantics* (Grand Rapids, 1983), pp. 141-43 and J.R. Firth, *Papers in Linguistics: 1934-1951* (London, 1957), pp. 194-214.

Some general issues										31

biblical world. The entry below for ἐξαίρω shows what
objects occur after the verb in sense 2.

ἐξαίρω: fut. ἐξαρῶ, pass. ἐξαρθήσομαι; aor. ἐξῆρα, inf.
ἐξᾶραι, pass. ἐξήρθην; pf.pass. ἐξῆρμαι.

1. to lift: τάλαντον μολίβου ἐξαιρόμενον Za 5.7.
2. to remove, get rid of, efface, obliterate, often of objects considered undesirable: the house of Jacob, Am 9.8; fortifications Mi 5.10 (// ἐξολεθρεύειν); city, Am 6.8; humans, Am 2.9, Ob 9,10, Na 2.1 (// συντελεῖσθαι), Ze 1.3 (// ἐκλείπειν), Za 10.2; kingdom of sinners, Am 9.8; tribe, Am 1.8 (// ἐξολεθρεύειν); θυσία καὶ σπονδή Jl 1.9, εὐφροσύνη καὶ χαρά Jl 1.9; ἀδικίας from one's consciousness, 'to overlook, take no notice of' Mi 7.18 (// ὑπερβαίνειν 'to pass over') Mi 7.18; χρεμετισμὸς ἵππων 'neighing of horses' Am 6.7; enemies, Na 1.2; hostile nations, Za 12.9; shepherds, Za 11.8; false prophets and an unclean spirit, ib.; fornication, Ho 2.2; τὸ αἷμα αὐτῶν ἐκ στόματος αὐτῶν καὶ τὰ βδελύγματα αὐτῶν ἐκ μέσου ὀδόντων αὐτῶν Za 9.7; objects associated with idolatry --- βωμοὶ Ὢν Ho 10.8, τὰ ὀνόματα τῆς Βααλ κ.τ.λ. Ze 1.4, sim. Ho 2.17, φάρμακα 'drugs' or 'charms' Mi 5.12 (v.l. ἐξολεθρεύσω).

The sphere from which an object is to be removed is expressed variously: ἀπὸ τῆς γῆς Za 13.2; ἀπὸ προσώπου τῆς γῆς Am 9.8, Ze 1.3; ἐκ προσώπου τινος Ho 2.2, Am 2.9; ἐκ στόματός τινος Ho 2.17, Jl 1.5, Za 5.7; ἐκ τοῦ τόπου Ze 1.4; ἐξ οἴκου τινος Jl 1.9; ἐκ τῶν χειρῶν τινος Mi 5.12; ἐκ μέσου τινος Za 9.7. Cf. αἴρω and ἐξολεθρεύω.

(9) הרם qal [1]; (14) כחד hi. [1]; (15) כרת b. ni.[4], c. hi.[3], d. ho.[1]; (19) נטל b. qal[1: Na 1.2, r > l, so Schleusner, s.v.]; (22) נסע c. ni.[1:

Za 10.2, voc.]; (23) נשׂא a. qal[1], b. ni.[1]; (27) סור a. qal[1], b. hi.[4: incl. Am 6.8, MT hsgrty]; (32) עבר hi. [1: so also Ez 20.39, MT ʿbdw]; (37) שמר a. ni.[1], b. hi.[4]; (fr.)[1: Am 1.8, MT twmk].

Under this heading one may usefully consider syntactical relationships such as the grammatical case of the object, what preposition mediates the verb and the object. Thus the use of ὅτι or διότι with γινώσκω is typical of its senses a and k.

c. SYNONYMIC AND ANTONYMIC RELATIONSHIPS IN PARALLELISM OR CONTRAST

Whilst to find a word joined by καί or ἤ does not necessarily permit us to establish that the two or more words so joined are synonymous or antonymous, it at least demonstrates that they belong to a single semantic field, even if in a rather loose sense. Furthermore, a word may be found with another in close proximity in a contrastive or antithetical relationship. It is for this reason that under γινώσκω a. we note cases of its parallelism with συνιέναι and ἐπιγινώσκειν. We wish to point out here that this sort of information is often not readily accessible through Hatch and Redpath's concordance, which does not provide a sufficiently large context. Therefore it is not methodologically sound to define senses of a word on the basis of a concordance. The latter can at best provide the necessary references, which must be studied in their full context.

Some general issues   33

3. **SEMANTIC FIELD**

In the post-Weisberger/Trier era one cannot engage in a semantic enquiry without taking into account the emphasis they laid on the notion of the field of semantically or ideationally associated words.[7] This approach is of course in line with the structuralist approach to linguistics as developped by F. de Saussure. Meanings and usage of a given word come into sharp relief when it is contrasted with an associated word or words, whilst the nature of such association can vary, synonymous, antonymous, contrastive, etc.[8]; see our observation at the end of the entry for ἥκω. For this reason we list at the bottom of many entries a word or words which form a semantic field with the entry word. This task is enormously helped by Xavier Jacques's *List of Septuagint Words Sharing Common Elements* (Rome, 1972), although his list is etymologically based; not all etymologically related words necessarily form a semantic field, and words which are not so related need to be added occasionally. Compare our entry for δοῦλος with that for δουλεύω; that for ἔρχομαι with that for ἥκω; and that for βλέπω with that for ὁράω. The comparison of the last two entries reveals that the verb βλέπω occurs always in a question in our corpus, and in two cases the answer to the question has ὁράω, i.e. ἑώρακα. Is this significant? Is βλέπω a complete synonym of ὁράω in these instances?

---

[7] See J. Lyons, *Semantics 1* (Cambridge, 1977), pp. 250-61. For a fine example of application of this approach, see now J.P. Louw and E.A. Nida (eds), *Greek-English Lexicon of the New Testament Based on Semantic Domains*, 2 vols., New York 1988.
[8] Some of these issues have been addressed above under 2 (b) 'Collocations.'

ἔρχομαι: aor. ἦλθον, inf. ἐλθεῖν.
The basic meaning is that of *coming to* or *arriving at* a focal point, whether the speaker himself or what looms large in his mind. Abs. and subst. ptc., ἐρχόμενος ἥξει 'one who is to come will arrive' Hb 2.3; + dat.pers. = dat.comm., *to become available for use or enjoyment* - ἕως τοῦ ἐλθεῖν γενήματα δικαιοσύνης ὑμῖν Ho 10.12; to assist, Za 9.9; + inf. of purpose, Ho 10.10, τί οὗτοι ἔρχονται ποιῆσαι; Za 1.21; + ἐπί τινα, with hostile intent, Am 4.2, Za 14.16. b. of a specific time or era, esp. in eschatological pronouncements: ἰδοὺ ἡμέραι ἔρχονται Am 4.2, 8.11, 9.13; sg. ἡμέρα Ma 4.1*bis*; ἡμέρα κυρίου Jl 3.31, Za 14.1, Ma 4.4. c. of a prayer, *to reach*, + πρός τινα Jn 2.8. d. *to originate*: πόθεν ἔρχῃ; 'where are you from?' Jn 1.8.

N.B. The pres. is sometimes used with fut. force: ἰδοὺ ἐγὼ ἔρχομαι καὶ κατασκηνώσω ἐν μέσῳ σου Za 2.10 (so all exs. in b. above), and cf. ἥξει ... ἰδοὺ ἔρχεται Ma 3.1.

ἥξω may be used as fut. of ἔρχομαι; ἐλεύσομαι is not attested in our corpus. Cf. δι~, εἰσ~, ἐξ~, ἐπ~, παρ~, προσ~, συνέρχομαι, πορεύομαι, ἀναβαίνω, βαδίζω, and ἥκω.

(5) בוא a. qal [21: incl. Ho 10.9 MT *b'wty*]. Del. Am 5.17, v.l. (v. s. διέρχομαι), 6.3, v.l.(v. s. εὔχομαι), 7.1, v.l.(v. s. ἄρχω), Za 12.9, v.l.(v. s. ἐπέρχομαι).

ἥκω: 3pl. ἥκασι (cf. Helbing, 103f.); fut. ἥξω. The pres. is used with the pf. force, whereas the fut. means "will come, arrive."

to have come, arrived: ἥκει τὸ πέρας ἐπὶ τὸν λαόν μου 'the end of my people has arrived' Am 8.2; of pers., Hg

Some general issues   35

2.7+; of God, Ho 6.3+; of days, Ho 9.7bis, Jl 1.15; ἐκδίκησις Mi 7.4; συντέλεια Hb 1.9; + dat.pers. Ho 13.13; + ἐπί τινα Mi 4.8, Am 8.2; + εἰς of destination - συντέλεια εἰς ἀσεβεῖς ἥξει 'an end will befall the infidel' Hb 1.9; + ἕως Mi 1.15, 4.10. b. fig., to reach a certain point: εἰς ὁμαλισμόν '(your cities) will eventually be levelled' Mi 7.12.

In contrast to ἔρχομαι, the verb emphasises the endpoint of the process of physical movement, thus 'to arrive': see esp. ἐρχόμενος ἥξει (not ἐλεύσεται) 'one who is to come will arrive' Hb 2.3. Cf. ἔρχομαι.

(1) אתה qal[1];   (2) בוא a. qal[22].

δουλεύω: 1aor. ἐδούλευσα.   †
to dutifully and obediently perform the duties incumbent upon oneself: + dat. pers., Za 2.9, of a son to his father, Ma 3.17; to God, αὐτῷ ὑπὸ ζυγὸν ἕνα Ze 3.9, Ma 3.14,18bis (// δίκαιος and [+ neg.] ἄνομος); ἐν γυναικί 'in return for a wife' Ho 12.12.

Cf. δοῦλος and δουλεία. What is prominent is not, despite the etymology, so much slavery and bondage as service.

(1) עבד a. qal [7].

δοῦλος, ου. m.   †
male slave, bondman: a. opp. κύριος '(human) master' --- υἱὸς δοξάζει πατέρα καὶ δ. τὸν κύριον αὐτοῦ Ma 1.6; + δούλη Jl 2.29   b. vis-à-vis the God of Israel --- Jn 1.9; applied to Moses, Ma 4.6; applied to a prophet, Am 3.7, Za 1.6, cf. Hg 2.23, Za 3.8. Cf. δούλη, δουλεύω, δεσπότης, παῖς, παιδίσκη, and κύριος. See Thackeray, Grammar, pp. 7-9 and Rengstorf in Kittel, 2.261-69; H.

Heinen, "Zur Terminologie der Sklaverei im ptolemäischen Ägypten," *Atti del XVII Congresso Internazional di Papirologia*, (Naples, 1984), pp. 1287-95.
(2) b. עָבַד [8: incl. Jn 1.9, r > d].

βλέπω. †
to perceive with the eyes, see (= ὁράω): all in a question --- τί σὺ βλέπεις (v.1. ὁρᾷς); Am 8.1, Za 4.2 (// ὁρᾶν), 5.2 (ὁρᾶν); πῶς ὑμεῖς βλέπετε αὐτόν; Hg 2.3. Cf. ὁράω, ἀνα~, ἀπο~, ἐπιβλέπω, and εἶδον.

(10) ראה a. qal[4]. Del. Na 2.9, v.1. (→ ἐπιβλέπω).

ὁράω: fut. ὄψομαι; pf. ἑώρακα (on the variant spelling ἑό~, e.g. in Za 1.8, see Helbing, 78, Mayser I.2.103, BDF, § 68, and Walters, 73. For the aor., εἶδον (q.v.) is used. †

1. *to perceive visually, see, notice*: abs., ὁ ὁρῶν Am 7.12; Mi 7.10,16, Za 1.8, 4.2,10, 9.5; τί σὺ ὁρᾷς; Am 7.8 (// τί σὺ βλέπεις; ib. 8.2, cf. Za 5.2); θαυμαστά Mi 7.15; σέ Na 3.7, Hb 3.10; τὴν δικαιοσύνην αὐτοῦ Mi 7.9; ἐν τοῖς ὀφθαλμοῖς μου Za 9.8; οἱ ὀφθαλμοὶ ὑμῶν Ma 1.5.
2. *to observe, look at*: οἱ ὁρῶντες τὰ ἐνύπνια Mi 3.7 (// μάντεις); of a shepherd, στήσεται καὶ ὄψεται καὶ ποιμανεῖ ib. 5.4; ὁράσεις Jl 2.28; πονηρά 'evil things' Hb 1.13 (// ἐπιβλέπειν); "they will behold their children and their hearts will rejoice" Za 10.7; ἀνὰ μέσον δικαίου καὶ ἀνὰ μέσον ἀνόμου Ma 3.18.
3. *to witness, experience*: οὐκ ὄψῃ κακὰ οὐκέτι Ze 3.15. Cf. ὅρασις, ὀπτασία, βλέπω, and εἶδον.

(5) חזה a. qal[2]; (8) ראה a. qal[20: incl. Mi 5.4,

‹ › ›; ib. 7.15; Ze 3.15 MT tyr'y]. Del. Am 8.2, v.l.(→ βλέπω); Za 12.10, v.l. (→ κόπτω).

4. UNIQUE SEPTUAGINTAL USAGE

This is by universal consent one of the most difficult and controversial aspects of Septuagintal lexicography. Before one can determine what is unique to Septuagintal usage, one needs to know exactly what is meant by the LXX text or what the translator intended it to mean as well as the range of usage attested outside of the LXX up to the Hellenistic period. Where one may suspect that one is dealing with a stereotype[9] or mechanical translation, the translator not really being concerned as to what the resultant rendering could have meant, the difficulty is especially acute.

Nevertheless, the general notion of Hebrew meanings and Greek words, or Semitism, is generally agreed to. The question boils down to particulars. For some examples which seem to us as evidencing such influence, see our entry for ἀναβαίνω 2, though here the papyrus example is most likely of the usual sense; δύναμαι; ἐκεῖνος (grammatical); ἰσχύς; ψυχή 3, where Ez 44.25 is most striking

---

[9] For a discussion on this issue, see E. Tov, "Three Dimensions of LXX words," *RB*, 83 (1976), 529-44; J.L.A. Lee, "Equivocal and stereotyped renderings in the LXX," *RB*, 87 (1980),104-17; and our study "Towards a Septuagint lexicon" in C.E. Cox (ed.), *VI Congress of the International Organization for Septuagint and Cognate Studies. Jerusalem 1986* [JBLSCS 23] (Atlanta, GA, 1987), pp. 255-76; and G. Dorival, M. Harl, and O. Munnich, *La Bible grecque des Septante. Du judaïsme hellénistique au christianisme ancien* (Paris, 1988), pp. 251-53.

in that the Greek word is used even for the Heb. מה, and it appears that this usage had already become part of the LXX vocabulary, most probably under the influence of passages such as Le 22.4 ὁ ἁπτόμενος πάσης ἀκαθαρσίας ψυχῆς for בכל־טמא־נפש הנגע and Nu 19.11 ὁ ἁπτόμενος τοῦ τεθνηκότος πάσης ψυχῆς ἀνθρώπου for הנגע במת לכל נפש אדם, and note also that Cyril of Alexandria understood our Haggai passage in the same spirit by referring to the ritual regulations in the Pentateuch; and finally (κατα)κληρονομέω.

δύναμαι: impf. ἠδυνάμην; 1aor. ἠδυνάσθην; fut. δυνήσομαι; subj.pres. δύνωμαι. The η- augment is better attested (cf. BDF, § 66, Th. § 16,3; Mayser, I.2.93f.); so is the "shorter" form (of Ionic origin) like ἠδυνάσθη as against ἠδυνήθη (e.g. Ho 12.4 v.l., and cf. Mayser, I.1.17, I.2.156, 158).

1. With inf., can, to be able (to): οὐκ ἠδυνάσθη ἰάσασθαι ὑμᾶς 'he was not able to cure you' Ho 5.13; ἕως τίνος οὐ μὴ δύνωνται καταρισθῆναι ib.8.5.

*2. abs., to prevail against, defeat: a. c. πρός τινα: ἠδυνάσθησαν πρός σε ἄνδρες εἰρηνικοί σου 'your allies prevailed against you' Ob 7; b. c. dat.pers., to prevail with: δυνήσομαι αὐτῷ (MT: אוכיל לא) Ho 11.4; c. c. μετά + gen.pers.: ἐνίσχυσε μετὰ ἀγγέλου καὶ ἠδυνάσθη 'he matched his strength with an angel and won' Ho 12.4.

This use (2), unknown outside of the LXX, is probably a Septuagintalism modelled on Hebrew יכל־ל, but could have developed from, and been understood in the light of, the classical sense 'to be equivalent to' (cf. Engl. to be equal to).

Cf. ἀδυναμία, ἀδυνατεῖν, ἀδύνατος, δύναμις, δυναστεία, δυνάστης, δυνατός, καταδυναστεία, καταδυναστεύειν, ἰσχύω, and κατισχύω.

(4) יכל   a. qal [9, including Ho 11.4]. Del. Ho 9.4, v.1.

ἐκεῖνος, η, ον.
Demonstrative pronoun with anaphoric force, *that*.
A. subst. and // οὗτος: οὗτοι ἐκείνοις προσθήσονται 'these will be added to those' Za 14.17.
B. adj., mostly in prophetic, eschatological sayings with ἐν τῇ ἡμέρᾳ ἐκείνῃ, ἐν ταῖς ἡμέραις ἐκείναις, or ἐν τῷ καιρῷ ἐκείνῳ; otherwise, λάλησον πρὸς τὸν νεανίαν ἐκεῖνον Za 2.4, παρατάξεται ἐν τοῖς ἔθνεσιν ἐκείνοις Za 14.3.

Both the prepositive and postpositive patterns are attested: ἐν ἐκείνῃ τῇ ἡμέρᾳ Ob 8 as against ἐν τῇ ἡμέρᾳ ἐκείνῃ Ho 1.5, the former 7 times in all, and the latter 54 times. Of the latter, no variant reading is recorded in this respect except in 16 cases. Since the postpositive pattern became increasingly popular in Ptolemaic papyri, the usage in our corpus cannot be entirely attributed to Hebrew influence; see BDF, § 292, Mayser, II.2.79-82, Th. 193. Note esp. Za 12.8 with both the patterns in a single verse.

On the other hand, the high frequency in our corpus of the adjectival use of the demonstrative with an articular noun is noteworthy in view of its marked infrequency in Ptolemaic papyri; see Mayser, II.2.79. Cf. οὗτος.

(6) הַהוּא, הַהִיא etc.[59]; (9) a. הָלַךְ [1]; (?) Za 14.17. Del. Za 13.8.

ἀναβαίνω: fut. ~βήσομαι; aor.subj. ~βῶ; aor.inf. ~βῆναι; aor.impv.3sg. ~βήτω. †
1. *to ascend, move up*. **a.** Physically, to a higher place: εἰς τὸν οὐρανόν Am 9.2 (opp. κατάγειν); ὡς ἄνδρες πολεμισταὶ ἀ. ἐπὶ τὰ τείχη 'like soldiers they will climb on to the walls' Jl 2.7, sim. 9; ἐπὶ τὸ ὄρος Hg 1.8. **b.** Heading for a more desirable destination: Na 2.8; ἐκ τῆς γῆς, poss. alluding to the Exodus, Ho 1.11; εἰς Ἀσσυρίους 'to Assyria' (in order to seek help) Ho 8.9; εἰς λαὸν παροικίας μου Hb 3.16. **c.** Up into a temple which is often situated on an elevated ground: εἰς τὸν οἶκον Ων Ho 4.15; εἰς τὸ ὄρος κυρίου καὶ εἰς τὸν οἶκον τοῦ θεοῦ Ιακωβ Mi 4.2; of an annual pilgrimage to Jerusalem, κατ' ἐνιαυτὸν τοῦ προσκυνῆσαι ... καὶ τοῦ ἑορτάζειν Za 14.16; εἰς Ιερουσαλημ, 17; 18*bis*,19. **d.** Of vegetation, 'to come up, shoot up': ἄκανθα καὶ τρίβολοι ἐπὶ τὰ θυσιαστήρια Ho 10.8; Jn 4.6. **e.** Of a foul odour rising: σαπρία, βρόμος Jl 2.20. **f.** Of a cry, clamour: κραυγή Jn 1.2. **g.** Embarking a ship: εἰς τὸ πλοῖον Jn 1.3 v.l. (for ἐμβαίνειν). **h.** Of mounting a horse: ἐφ' ἵππον Ho 14.4; ἱππέως ἀναβαίνοντος Na 3.3. **i.** Of a threatening object or person with a hostile intent: abs. Jl 3.9; ἀ. ὡς ποταμὸς συντέλεια Am 8.8, 9.9 (// καταβαίνειν) --- on the use in papyri of this verb on the flooding of the Nile, see Preisigke, s.v.; of an army setting out on a military campaign, ἐπὶ τὴν γῆν μου 'advance against my land' Jl 1.6; 3.12; τοῦ ἐκδικῆσαι, of a punitive action, Ob 21; εἰς πρόσωπόν σου Na 2.2.
*2. *to go away*: ἀναβήτω φθορὰ ζωῆς μου 'may the decay of my life be removed!' Jn 2.7 (MT: /taʻal mīššaḥat ḥayyay/). On this semantic development, cf. עלה ni. and MH/Jewish Aramaic *slq* 'to ascend' > *hstlq* 'to disappear, go away', and MM, s.v., cite a papyrus ex. (iii B.C.) πλήρωμα ἀναβέβηκεν 'the gang has gone away.' But this

usage is unknown to Preisigke.

Cf. καταβαίνω, ἐμβαίνω, ἐπιβαίνω and ἀναβιβάζω.

(11) עלה a. qal [26], c. hi. [2], d. ho [1];(16) רכב qal [1]. Del. (5) ירד qal, Jn 1.3 v.l., Hg 2.23 v.l.; (10) עבר qal Am 5.5 v.l.

ἰσχύς, ύος, f. †
1. *strength*: a. in general - ἔθετο ἀγάπησιν κραταιὰν ~ος αὐτοῦ Hb 3.4; ἐν τῇ ~ύι ἡμῶν 'with our own strength', i.e. with nobody's help, Am 6.13; see also Hb 1.11; God's strength, ἐν ('relying on') ~ύι κυρίου Mi 5.4, μεγάλη ἡ ἰ. αὐτοῦ (i.e. κυρίου) Na 1.3. b. *physical, bodily strength*, ἡ ἰ. σου ἀνδρὸς πειρατοῦ 'your strength is that of a brigand' Ho 6.9; ἀνδρίσαι τῇ ~ύι σφόδρα 'play the man well' Na 2.2; // δύναμις, and opp. a divine spirit, Za 4.6; // ὀχύρωμα 'fortress' and opp. συντριμμός 'ruin' Am 5.9; // θαυμαστά 'marvels, wonders' Mi 7.13; ὁ κραταιὸς οὐ μὴ κρατήσῃ ~ος αὐτοῦ 'the strong will not maintain his strength' Am 2.14. c. *military might* to rely on: Αἰθιοπία ἡ ἰ. αὐτῆς Na 3.9.
*d. w. ref. to agricultural produce, fruit as a manifestation of power inherent in plants: ἄμπελος καὶ συκῆ ἔδωκαν τὴν ~ὺν αὐτῶν 'the vine and fig-tree have yielded their fruits' Jl 2.22.
2. *innate ability* to do sth: δράγμα οὐκ ἔχον ~ὺν τοῦ ποιῆσαι ἄλευρον 'a sheaf of corn which does not have the capability of yielding meal' Ho 8.7.
*3. *wealth, material possessions* as an indication of one's strength (cf. s.v. δύναμις, 2): consisting in a vast quantity of gold, silver and robes, Za 14.14; // πλῆθος 'abundance' Mi 4.13; κατέφαγον ἀλλότριοι τὴν ~ὺν αὐτοῦ 'strangers devoured his wealth' Ho 7.9; κατάξει ἐκ

σου ~ύν σου Am 3.11 (of wealth laid up in an elevated fortress? Or possibly of troops high up in a fortress --- cf. Cyr. I.432). Cf. δύναμις, κράτος, δύναμαι, ἰσχύω, and κατισχύω.

(5) גְבוּרָה [1]; (12) c. חֵזֶק [1]; (13) חַיִל [3]; (16) חֹם [8: add Ho 6.9 voc.]; (21) b. עֹל [4: add Am 5.9 voc.]; (22) b. עֹצֶם [1: Na 3.9 voc.]. Del. Hb 3.16 (v.l.), and (24) עָצְמָה Ho 8.7 fr.

ψυχή. ῆς. f. †
1. *physical life*: of a human, Jn 1.14; + λαμβάνειν 'to take life, kill' Ho 4.8 (on which see *AJBI* 9 ['83] 36-38), Jn 4.3; + σῴζειν. Am 2.14,15; ἀπελέγετο τὴν ~ἠν αὐτοῦ 'he felt like giving up on his own life' Jn 4.8.
2. *man's immaterial, inner existence and strength*: περιεχύθη μοι ὕδωρ ἕως ~ῆς 'water was poured round me, reaching my soul' Jn 2.6; "as my inner strength was about to fail me" Jn 2.8.   a. involved in moral, ethical aspects --- ἁμαρτία ~ῆς μου Mi 6.7, cf. ἐξήμαρτεν ἡ ψ. σου Hb 2.10; b. desire καταθύμιον ~ῆς αὐτοῦ 'his inner desire' ib. 7.3; ἐπλάτυνε καθὼς ὁ ᾅδης τὴν ~ἠν αὐτοῦ Hb 2.5.   c. intellectual, emotional reaction --- οὐκ εὐδοκεῖ ἡ ψ. μου ἐν αὐτῷ 'I am not pleased with him' Hb 2.4; ταραχθῆναι τὴν ~ἠν μου ἐν ὀργῇ Hb 3.2; εἰρήνη ~ῆς 'inner peace' Hg 2.9; βαρυνθήσεται ἡ ψ. μου ἐπ' αὐτούς, καὶ γὰρ αἱ ~αἱ αὐτῶν ἐπωρύοντο ἐπ' ἐμέ 'I shall be gravely distressed over them, for their souls howled at me' Za 11.8.
*3. *corpse*: Hg 2.13 (so Cyr. II.272, and cf. Ez 44.25 ψ. = MT *mēt*).([10])

([10]) Harl, op. cit., pp. 249f., holds that this is due to the ellipsis of the (participial) adjective τετελευτηκυῖα, but 'deceased soul' is not the same as 'corpse.'

Some general issues   43

*4.   a Hebraic substitute for a reflexive pronoun: οἱ
ἄρτοι αὐτῶν ταῖς ψυχαῖς αὐτῶν '... for themselves, for
their own enjoyment' Ho 9.4.

Cf. καρδία and πνεῦμα.

(4) נפשׁ [18];   (-) [2]. Del. Hg 2.14a, v.1.

κατακληρονομέω: fut. ~ήσω.   †
1. to take possession of, following a successful military operation, + acc. rei: a land or a part of it, Am 2.10, Ob 19bis; σκηνώματα Hb 1.6.
*2. to dispossess, + acc. pers.: ~μήσουσιν ὁ οἶκος Ιακωβ τοὺς ~μήσαντας αὐτούς Ob 17.   ***3. to make, appoint as one's heir:** ~ κύριος τὸν Ιουδαν τὴν μερίδα αὐτοῦ ἐπὶ τὴν γῆν ἁγίαν 'the Lord will appoint Judah his portion as heir over (= of) the holy land' Za 2.12 (cf. Th. Sp. 339 ὅς τῷ τε Ιουδα τὴν παλαιὰν αὐτῷ μερίδα τῆς γῆς ἀποδώσει).(¹¹)
4. to give as possession (τινί τι): τοῖς καταλοίποις τοῦ λαοῦ μου πάντα ταῦτα '... all these things [= natural resources]' Za 8.12.

Cf. κληρονομέω.

(3) ירשׁ a. qal [5],   b. hi. [1: Ob 17b, voc.];   (5) נחל a. qal [1],   c. hi. [1].

(¹¹) Za 2.12 καὶ κατακληρονομήσει κύριος τὸν Ιουδαν τὴν μερίδα αὐτοῦ ἐπὶ τὴν γῆν τὴν ἁγίαν καὶ αἱρετιεῖ ἔτι τὴν Ιερουσαλημ for MT (2.16) /wnāḥal yhwh ʾet yhudā ḥelqō ʿal ʾadmat haqqōdeš uvāḥar ʿōd bîrušālayim/. This seems to me to be a reasonable interpretation. To make τὴν μερίδα appositional to Ιουδαν is difficult because of ἐπὶ τὴν γῆν ...

κληρονομέω: fut. -ήσω. †
1. *to take possession of*: τὸ ἀργύριον αὐτῶν ὄλεθρος ~ 'destruction [= hostile, destructive troops?] will inherit their silver' Ho 9.6; cities Ob 20. *2. *to dispossess*, + acc. pers.: Ze 2.9 (// διαρπάζειν 'to plunder'), Za 9.4.
Cf. κατακληρονομέω. On the fact that the word group κληρονόμος in the LXX often signifies, no doubt under the Hebrew influence, violent appropriation rather than peaceful transfer of property upon someone's natural death, see esp. Foerster in Kittel, 3.776-79, and also G. Dalman, *Die Worte Jesu* (Leipzig, ²1930), pp. 102f. Note, for instance, the use of κληρονομεῖν with ref. to Ahab's appropriation of Naboth's vineyard on the latter's "death" (3Ki 21.15-19).

(5) ירשׁ *a.* qal [2], *b.* hi. [1]; (7) נחל *a.* qal [1].

5. GRAPPLING WITH LXX AS A GREEK DOCUMENT

Notwithstanding one's recognition of the basic character of the LXX for most of its parts as a work of translation, it is equally important to recognise that the LXX *is* a Greek document, and one must attempt to read it as such, and it has been so read down the ages. Even such a book as Qoheleth with its well-known Aquilanic traits has been so read by Gregory Thaumatourgos, who produced a paraphrastic commentary([12]) on it without ever referring to oddities of its Greek. Before one concludes, out of despair perhaps, that a particular rendition is merely an attempt mechanically to reproduce the Hebrew, every

---

([12]) On this commentary see a recent Melbourne University doctoral dissertation: J. Jarick, Gregory Thaumatourgos' Paraphrase of Ecclesiastes, 1988.

attempt ought to be made to comprehend the translation as a Greek document. Here, in addition to Classical sources and non-Septuagintal, Hellenistic sources, we have found it useful to study how the LXX was understood by New Testament writers, patristic commentators([13]) and those who produced daughter versions from it.([14])

To illustrate the point, see our entry for ἀποβλέπω, especially with reference to Ma 3.9 καὶ ἀποβλέποντες ἀποβλέπετε, καὶ ἐμὲ ὑμεῖς πτερνίζετε for MT /bamm'ērā 'attem nē'ārim w'ōti 'attem qōv'im/ "you are accursed with curse". Generally speaking, that the verb has these two diametrically opposed meanings is an assured fact, and it is an understandable semantic process. What makes our judgement on Ma 3.9 difficult is that the verb is used absolutely without any prepositional complement. A variant reading with εἰς αὐτά, the pron. apparently referring back to "the tithes," is probably an attempt to interpret the verb in sense 1, and Th. 424 with ἐπί τινα μεγίστην ὠφέλειαν ἀφορῶντες is in the same spirit, whereas the Eth's use of the verb taʿawwara "he neglected, despised" attests to sense 2.

ἀποβλέπω. †
    to turn attention (to ἐπί + acc.): ἐπὶ θεοὺς ἀλλοτρίους 'on alien gods' Ho 3.1. 2. to turn attention away, disregard: ἀποβλέποντες ἀποβλέπετε Ma 3.9.
    Cf. βλέπω.

([13]) Where Migne's Patrologia Graeca is not used, we cite Cyril of Alexandria from the ed. by P.E. Pusey (Oxford, 1868) and Theodor of Mopsuestia from the ed. by H.N. Sprenger, *Theodori Mopsuesteni Commentarius in XII Prophetas* (Wiesbaden, 1977).
([14]) See G. Dorival et al. (n. 9 above), p. 252.

(4) a. ראה qal [1: Ma 3.9 MT n'rym > r'ym], b. מַרְאֶה
[1: Ma 3.9 MT m'rh > mr'h].

Another intriguing case is that of θυσία. In some of its occurrences, the word possibly means *cultic offering in general*, i.e. including vegetable and meal offerings, esp. where its hyponym is /minḥā/, which covers both meat and non-meat offerings. Indeed, θυσία is the main LXX rendition of this Heb. word, δῶρον being a much less common equivalent. Note especially that in the first LXX occurrences of the hyponym in Genesis 4, the LXX uses θυσία for Cain's offering, though his was not a meat offering, whereas Abel's *minḥā*, which one would have expected to be rendered with θυσία, is actually rendered δῶρα. The fact that a derivative of the Greek word, θυσιαστήριον, has become the standard rendition of /mizbēaḥ/, where both types of offering were placed, may have contributed to this possibly ambiguous usage in the LXX. No such ambiguity seems to be known outside of the Biblical corpus and the literature influenced by it.[15] It is a fact that the LXX translators did use the word in the broad sense as proven by an example such as Le 5.13 ἡ θυσία τῆς σεμιδάλεως for MT *hamminḥā*. Classical Greek seems to lack a word for 'cereal offering' as such.

θυσία, ας. f. †

animal sacrifice offered as part of a cultic institution: Ho 3.4; 6.6 (// ὁλοκαύτωμα), Ma 1.8; Za 9.1; κυρίου Ze 1.8, cf. ib. 1.7, 3.10; cogn. obj. of θύειν, Ho 8.13, Jn 1.16; pl. Ho 9.4 (// οἶνος), Am 4.4,

---

[15] Cf. S. Daniel, *Recherches sur le vocabulaire du culte dans la Septante* (Paris, 1965), pp. 203, 209f.

Some general issues   47

5.25; as obj. of φέρειν Am 5.22 (+ ὁλοκαύτωμα), Ma 1.13;
of προσφέρειν Am 4.4, 5.25 (// σφάγιον); of προσάγειν Ma
2.12, 3.3; of προσδέχεσθαι Ma 1.10;   ἐπιβλέπειν εἰς ~αν
Ma 2.13; καθαρὰ θ. Ma 1.11 (// θυμίαμα); ἀρέσει τῷ κυρίῳ
θ. Ιουδα καὶ Ιερουσαλημ Ma 3.4; // σπονδή Jl 1.9,13,
2.14.   Cf. θύω and θυσιάζω.

(2) חבר a. qal[1], b. חָבֵר [8];   (4) מחֲנֶה [14: incl.
Za 9.1, voc.].

Finally, περιοχή in Ob 1 is another difficult case. The
LXX reads: Ἀκοὴν ἤκουσα παρὰ κυρίου, καὶ περιοχὴν εἰς τὰ
ἔθνη ἐξαπέστειλεν ... for MT /šmuʿā šāmaʿnu mēʾet yhwh
wṣir baggōyim šullāḥ.../. The Greek noun, derived from
περιέχω, has something to do with encircling. Two Greek
commentators, Theodor and Cyril, seem to have understood
it to mean something like a besieging army.[16]

περιοχή. ῆς. f. †
siege: ἔσται π. ἐπὶ Ιερουσαλημ Za 12.2; ὕδωρ ~ῆς 'water
supplies at a time of siege'(?) Na 3.14; ~ὴν (MT ṣ(r)
εἰς τὰ ἔθνη ἐξαπέστειλεν 'he dispatched a besieging army
to the nations'(?) Ob 1 (so Th. 161 and Cyr. I.549).

(3) a. צור qal [1: Ob 1], מָצוֹר [2].

---

[16] Theodor of Mopsuestia: Περιοχὴν λέγει τὸ κύκλῳ τι
περιέχον, οἷον τεῖχος ἤ τι τοιοῦτο ... ὥσπερ τινα περιοχὴν
τὸ πρόσταγμα ἐξαπέστειλε τὸ οἰκεῖον εἰς τὰ ἔθνη ὁ θεός,
ἅπαντας αὐτοὺς ἐν κύκλῳ κατὰ τῆς Ιδουμαίας συλλέγων ...τοῦ
θεοῦ ... κελεύοντος, καὶ πανταχόθεν ἐπ' αὐτὴν τὰ ἔθνη
συλλέγοντος ...
    Cyril of Alexandria: Κατ' αὐτῶν γὰρ ἀπεστάλθαι φησὶ
τὴν περιοχήν, ἤτοι πολιορκίαν, ἤγουν τὸν συγκλεισμόν...

ΑΓΑΠΑΝ IN THE SEPTUAGINT

S.P. Swinn

The vocabulary of 'love' in the LXX(¹) is a subject of interest to students both of the LXX and also of the NT. There are various reasons for this. So dominant a theme in both OT and NT can hardly fail to call for notice; and the important place occupied by the LXX in the worship and thought of Jews and Christians in the first century compels the student of the NT to weigh up LXX evidence in his or her interpretation of the NT. However, the intrinsic importance of the subject is made all the more acute by differences which are clearly visible between Classical Greek 'love' terminology and that of the LXX/NT.

The notoriety of the last point has caused some rather bold claims in explanation; and before going on to look at the LXX vocabulary itself it is necessary briefly to sketch the issue and also to establish a method of addressing it.

(¹) Two terms need clarification at the outset. (1) 'Love' is used in this paper to refer to the class of words, ἀγαπᾶν, φιλεῖν, etc., though their meanings are not restricted to a single definition. (2) LXX refers properly only to the OG (= Old Greek) Pentateuch; however, it is used here to refer to the text of Rahlfs' 1935 edition of the Greek OT. Rahlfs' text is not without its defects (cf. R.W. Klein, *Textual Criticism of the Old Testament: The Septuagint after Qumran* [Philadelphia: Fortress, 1974], p. 54); but where there is doubt about a reading, reference has generally been made to the larger editions or commentaries.

THE PROBLEM

The problem may be summarised thus. In ancient Greek, various verbs existed to express the idea 'love'. The four most prominent were φιλεῖν, ἐρᾶν, στέργειν and ἀγαπᾶν; but in fifth-century Classical Greek the most general (outside erotic contexts) was φιλεῖν. When one looks at the LXX and NT, the scene is rather different: not only are ἐρᾶν and στέργειν almost non-existent in both LXX and NT, but the incidence of ἀγαπᾶν vastly outweighs that of φιλεῖν. Moreover, the LXX is the first place in Greek literature where a new noun for 'love', ἀγάπη, is attested; yet ἀγάπη rises to singular prominence in the NT.

Can it be that for some reason Judaeo-Christian usage determinedly adopted and developed one of the rarer words for 'love', whilst leaving aside the everyday terminology?

W. Barclay is typical of many who would answer that question in the affirmative, positing a theological motivation for the change:(²)

(²) A rather different view is that of G.B. Caird ('Homoeophony in the Septuagint', *Jews, Greeks and Christians: Religious Cultures in Late Antiquity* [Essays in honour of W.D. Davies, ed. R. Hamerton-Kelly & R. Scroggs; Leiden, 1976], pp. 80-83), who, claiming that ἀγαπᾶν and ἀγάπη were 'apparently current but not common in classical and hellenistic Greek', attributed their frequency in the LXX to their mere resemblance in *sound* to the Hebrew אהב and אהבה. Given, however, the evidence developed in this paper -- and given that אהב and ἀγαπᾶν, to say the least, do not *differ* in meaning -- Caird's hypothesis must be viewed as fanciful. (If he were correct, how would departures from ἀγαπᾶν such as in Ge 37.4 be explained?) My own study of hom(oe)ophony in the LXX shows it to be a rather less frequent phenomenon than Caird suggests; see also E. Tov, "Loan-words, Homophony and Transliterations in the Septuagint", *Bib* 60 (1979)

It is true to say that all the other words had acquired certain flavours which made them unsuitable '... Christian thought fastened on this word *agapē* because it was the only word capable of being filled with the content which was required.(³)

Similarly E. Stauffer:

> The LXX almost always renders the אהב of the Hebrew text by ἀγαπᾶν ... Ἔρως and φιλία and derivatives are strongly suppressed. The harmless ἀγαπᾶν carries the day, mainly because by reason of its prior history it is the best adapted to express the thoughts of selection, of willed address and of readiness for action. But the true victor in the competition is the ancient אהב, which impresses on the colourless Greek word its own rich and strong meaning.(⁴)

The above works have both been very influential in Christian circles. As recently as 1986, G.A. Turner writes in similar vein:

> Those who translated the OT into Greek ignored the common Greek term for love (*érōs*) because of its sensual associations and chose instead the obscure term *agápē* to translate Heb. 'ā́hab and its synonyms.

(footnote 2 continued)
216-238; J. Barr, *The Typology of Literalism in Ancient Bilical Translations* [Göttingen, 1979], p. 45). [See also J. Barr, "Doubt about homoeophony in the Septuagint", *Textus* 12 (1985) 1-77, esp. 65f. - Ed.]
(³) Barclay, *New Testament Words* (London: SCM, 1964), p. 20.
(⁴) G. Quell & E. Stauffer, "ἀγαπάω", *TWNT* 1 (1957) p. 39; or *ThDNT* 1 (1964), p. 39.

Erōs passed from the scene as the Judeo-Christian influence became dominant; ... In contrast to *érōs* with its inclusiveness, Heb. *'āhab* and its Greek counterpart *agápē* stress exclusiveness, specifically God's love for His chosen people.(⁵)

However, against such a strong array of opinion, a call for its advocates to prove their case must be registered. Put simply, *what factual evidence is there that Judaeo-Christian usage chose a less than usual* Greek word to express the meaning 'love'? The question is *not* whether 'love' in the Bible has a richer meaning than in pagan thought, but whether its *terminology* is in and of itself distinct. Even before ancient Greek evidence is considered, the evidence of Modern Greek suggests *a priori* that the terminology itself was not in fact distinct. For in Modern Greek, the ordinary noun for 'love' is ἀγάπη, φιλία only meaning 'friendship' ; and the ordinary verb for 'love' is ἀγαπᾶν -- φιλεῖν means 'kiss', 'embrace', but it does not mean 'love'.(⁶)

The thesis of this paper is that the 'love' terminology of the LXX (and hence also of the NT) reflects the actual usage of the time and can be located on the plane of development from Classical to Modern Greek.(⁷) As well as noting evidence for that development, it will be shown that the LXX itself points to the same conclusion. It is beyond the scope of this paper to explore the

---

(⁵) G.A. Turner, 'Love', *International Standard Bible Encyclopaedia* (rev., ed. G.W. Bromiley; 4 vols.; Grand Rapids, 1979-1988), vol. 3, p. 175.

(⁶) C.C. Tarelli, "'ΑΓΑΠΗ", *JTS*, NS 1 (1950) 65-66.

(⁷) Not, however, to deny that the NT writers 'gave a new breadth and length and depth and height of meaning to the idea of love' (Tarelli, art. cit., 66).

theological implications of the argument; but readers are urged to recognise that it is *context*, and not the prior history of the vocabulary, which gives richness to the ideas of a given passage; only in cases where deliberate allusion to earlier usage can be recognised is it legitimate to import dimensions from the latter, aside from establishing the basic meanings and collocations of the words.

THE EVIDENCE OF EXTERNAL USAGE

There clearly was some distinction between the terms for 'love' in classical Greek; but Stauffer is oversimplifying the case when he writes that ἀγαπᾶν has 'nothing of the power or magic of ἐρᾶν and little of the warmth of φιλεῖν':([8]) later, he himself adds that it is often used merely as a synonym of ἐρᾶν or φιλεῖν, so that its meaning "is still imprecise, and its individuation still tentative,... '.([9]) LSJ state briefly that ἀγαπᾶν is used "as dist. fr. φιλέω (q.v.) implying regard rather than affection, but the two are interchanged, cf. X. *Mem.* 2.7.9 and 12; ... '.

The capacity for distinction between terms for 'love' may be seen, for example, in Aristotle, *Rhet.* 1371ᵃ 21: τὸ δὲ φιλεῖσθαι ἀγαπᾶσθαι ἐστιν αὐτὸν δι᾽ αὐτόν.([10]) Compare

---

([8]) Stauffer, "ἀγαπάω", p. 36.
([9]) Ibid. p. 37.
([10]) R. Joly (*Le vocabulaire chrétien de l'amour est-il original?* Φιλεῖν et 'Αγαπᾶν dans le grec antique [Bruxelles, 1968], pp. 38-39) points out that this line is often wrongly understood. Tarelli (" 'ΑΓΑΠΗ", 67) states that 'ἀγαπάω in the New Testament corresponds much more closely to Aristotle's φιλέω than to his ἀγαπάω.'

also his reference to φιλία ἄνευ τοῦ στέργειν (*Eth.Nic.* 1126ᵇ22), in the case of two of the other words. On the other hand, overlap in usage can be seen by examining the range of definitions exhibited in the lexica. For instance, στέργειν, φιλεῖν and ἀγαπᾶν can all be used of the love of parents for children; and all three words are used (if seldom) with reference to sexual love.([11]) Part of this is attributable to developments which took place over the course of time; but it is significant that LSJ cite examples from the Classical period, demonstrating that the synonymity was established well before the Koine period.([12]) Plutarch's use of ἀγαπᾶν in reference to foreigners on a visit to Rome 'caressing' their pet monkeys and puppies (*Per.* 1) has been cited as an example of the coldness of ἀγαπᾶν by comparison with φιλεῖν, but this is very doubtful in the context of the passage.([13])

Enough has been said to illustrate the overlap of terms in 'pagan' Greek. However, there is plentiful evidence to show that ἀγαπᾶν was gradually taking the place of the other words for 'love'. The best discussion of this is found in an important monograph by the Belgian

---

([11]) LSJ note ἀγαπᾶν ἑταίραν, Anaxil. 22.1; but ἀγαπᾶν ἑταίρας 'to be fond of them', Xen. *Mem.* 1.5.4. Cf. perh. also ἡ ἀγαπωμένη 'sweetheart' in Luc., *J.Tr.* 2, in the context of ἔρως 'love' and ἐρωτικόν 'love-affair'.

([12]) E.g., ἀγαπᾶν (especially in Attic: cf. LSJ, s.v., III) and στέργειν (Soph., *OC* 7; Demosth. 18.122) both mean 'be content', 'be satisfied'.

([13]) Barclay (*Words*, p.19) regards it as cold; but Plutarch reports that Caesar admonished the foreigners for wasting on their pets affection (τὸ φύσει φιλητικὸν ... καὶ φιλόστοργον) due properly to their children (παιδία) or fellow humans (ἀνθρώποις).

scholar Robert Joly.(14)

It was not until after completing a study on ἀγαπᾶν in the LXX a number of years ago that the writer came across Joly's discussion; however, he was gratified to find that both had come to essentially identical conclusions. Joly's work, both for the soundness of his methodology and for his extensive research into Classical and post-Classical Greek writings, deserves a more than passing reference here.

Joly challenges head-on the popular view which sees a 'linguistic reversal' in the Greek vocabulary of love between pagan writers and the LXX/NT: although such a reversal is regularly affirmed, it has never been proved.(15)

The reader must be left to pursue for himself the details of Joly's case, in particular his documentation,(16) but his broad argument is that the shift from φιλεῖν to ἀγαπᾶν was a development not of the LXX or NT writers but of ordinary Greek usage well before the time of the LXX.(17) Nor was the change simply on the level of popular speech: for the decline of φιλεῖν can be clearly

---

(14) See n. 10 above. I am grateful to Dr J.A.L. Lee, who first drew my attention to it. Joly's monograph is framed in response to writings by B.B. Warfield ("The terminology of love in the New Testament", *Princeton Theological Review* 16 [1918] 1-45, 153-203) and esp. C. Spicq (*Agapè dans le Nouveau Testament: Analyse des Textes* [3 vols.; Paris, 1958-59]). A more recent work which I have unfortunately not seen is J. Barr, *The Vocabulary of Love in the Greek Bible* (Grinfield Lectures, 1978).

(15) Joly, *Vocabulaire*, p. 10.

(16) Some of Joly's material is diffuse and was not easy to summarise. I have not checked all his references, which partly overlapped with my own.

(17) *Vocabulaire*, p. 48.

seen in Greek literature of the fourth century B.C.[18]

Readers who have not read Joly may wonder how debate could exist over what must surely be a question of fact. However, the problem arises from a series of illusions regarding the commonness of φιλεῖν which few have thought to challenge.[19]

Partly to blame here is the Classical background from which most of us come to the study of Koine. Joly points out that we meet φιλεῖν either as a paradigm for the -έω verb or at least as a vocabulary item in early prose composition exercises. Most of the literature which we read after that comes from the fifth century B.C. or earlier, when φιλεῖν was still the current verb for 'love' aside from erotic contexts.[20]

Even when reading writers of the fourth century B.C., we fail to discern the shift which is taking place, because of a number of factors:

1. The decline in use of φιλεῖν only affected its meaning 'love'; its other meanings continued long in antiquity ('be wont') or up to the present day ('kiss').[21]

2. φιλεῖν's decline was gradual, not complete even by NT times; some Greek writers emphatically preferred it to ἀγαπᾶν.[22]

3. As an antonym of μισεῖν, φιλεῖν enjoyed a certain degree of favour (though ἀγαπᾶν is also frequently found),

---

[18] In this statement, Joly (op. cit., p. 49) moves beyond the positions of Warfield and Tarelli (" 'ΑΓΑΠΗ").
[19] See esp. Joly, *Vocabulaire*, pp. 30-31.
[20] See op. cit., p. 15.
[21] 'Love', 'be wont', mainly in a limited conjugation; 'kiss' in a full conjugation (op. cit., p. 27).
[22] See op. cit., pp. 20, 24, 26 (slight, passing literary revival of φιλεῖν around NT times), 29.

no doubt because of similarities in sound between the pair of verbs -- the same number of syllables, the same paradigm.(²³)

4. In philosophical discussions of φιλία, φιλεῖν was the natural verb to use.(²⁴)

5. When a writer quoted from an earlier writer who used φιλεῖν, the later writer would himself naturally use φιλεῖν in the context.

6. In letters, φιλεῖν was the regular term in two frequent epistolary formulas: ἀσπάζομαι τοὺς φιλοῦντάς σε πάντας κατ' ὄνομα and τὸ προσκύνημα πάντων τῶν φιλούντων με. Those account between them for most of the occurrences of φιλεῖν -- much more frequent than ἀγαπᾶν -- in the documentary papyri; the fact that they were standard formulas shows the danger of drawing hasty conclusions from them about the current usage of the day.(²⁵)

7. The cognates φίλος, φιλία and φιλο- in compounds do not suffer any decline; but note equally that they have no synonyms derived from the stem ἀγαπ-.

8. Where scholars have made statistical studies of the use of ἀγαπᾶν in non-Biblical writers, they have frequently neglected to compile (and especially to evaluate) statistics on the occurrence of φιλεῖν too, and so they have been led to wrong conclusions.(²⁶)

Joly's detailed analysis of the vocabulary for love in writers from the fifth century B.C. to the post-NT period demonstrates clearly that φιλεῖν is declining in use and is being replaced by ἀγαπᾶν;(²⁷) a strength of his case is that he is able to provide a linguistic explanation for

---

(²³) Ibid., p. 11.   (²⁴) Ibid., p. 18.
(²⁵) Ibid., pp. 27-29.
(²⁶) Ibid., pp. 10-22. Evaluation is important: see Joly's discussion of Aristotle (p. 19) and Strabo (p. 22).
(²⁷) Cf. the whole of his chap. 2 (pp. 10-29).

the change. He argues that it was the meaning of φιλεῖν 'kiss' which killed its meaning 'love'. The former is not evident in literature before the fifth century B.C., yet the decline of the latter can be discerned in the next century; Joly maintains that it was the embarrassing potential for ambiguity which brought about its decline-- he posits a connection between the rise of φιλεῖν 'kiss' and the decline of the verb κυνεῖν -- he suggests that the latter occurred because of an embarrassing "collision homonymique" with the aorist active of κύειν.(28) The theory makes good sense and readily shows why the meaning 'be wont', and also the meaning 'love' (i) in opposition to μισεῖν, (ii) as a technical term in discussing φιλία and (iii) in epistolary formulas, survived longer: they were all linguistically more solid than φιλεῖν 'love' in general.(29)

Finally, Joly points out an inherent weakness in the verb φιλεῖν itself: although the verbs ἀγαπᾶν, στέργειν and ἐρᾶν each had a substantival counterpart with the meaning 'love' (ἀγάπησις / ἀγάπη, στοργή and ἔρως), φιλεῖν had no such counterpart -- φιλία properly meant 'friendship', not 'love' -- and that must have caused some awkwardness for the Greeks.(30)

Lest it be thought that Joly's argument is too inge-

---

(28) Op. cit., pp. 31-34 (quoting Gilliéron).
(29) Ibid., p. 34. (The reference to epistolary formulas is mine.) A further sense developed by φιλεῖν, as a euphemism for βαίνειν or βινεῖν (see G.P. Shipp, *Modern Evidence for Ancient Greek Vocabulary* [Sydney, 1979] pp. 126f.), would hardly favour its continued use as a general verb for 'love'.
(30) *Vocabulaire*, p. 34. Joly (p. 47) points out that φιλία and φίλος were not affected by the decline of φιλεῖν 'love', because they were semantically quite distinct.

nious, it should be emphasised that it accords with the evidence. To take only three of his examples, who can seriously question that ἀγαπᾶν and φιλεῖν are being used interchangeably in the following? --

> Dionysius of Halicarnassus, *Ant.Rom.* 8.34 (I B.C.):
> φιλοῦμέν τε ἅπαντες τὰ ὠφελοῦντα καὶ μισοῦμεν τὰ βλάπτοντα ... πόλιν τε τὴν γειναμένην ἡμᾶς, ὅταν μὲν ὠφελῇ, στέργομεν, ὅταν δὲ βλάπτῃ, καταλείπομεν, οὐ διὰ τὸν τόπον ἀγαπῶντες αὐτήν, ἀλλὰ διὰ τὸ συμφέρον.
> Plotinus, 2.9.16 (III A.D.): ὁ τὸ φιλεῖν πρὸς ὁτιοῦν ἔχων καὶ τὸ συγγενὲς πᾶν οὗ φιλεῖ ἀσπάζεται καὶ τοὺς παῖδας ὧν τὸν πατέρα ἀγαπᾷ.
> Xenophon, *Mem.* 2.7.9,12 (IV B.C.): σὺ μὲν ἐκείνας φιλήσεις ὁρῶν ὠφελίμους σεαυτῷ οὔσας, ἐκεῖναι δέ σε ἀγαπήσουσιν αἰσθόμεναι χαίροντά σε αὐταῖς. ... καὶ αἱ μὲν ὡς κηδεμόνα ἐφίλουν, ὁ δὲ ὡς ὠφελίμους ἠγάπα.

In each case, the variation cannot be more than stylistic.[31]

That leads, then, to the most serious of Joly's conclusions: if ἀγαπᾶν is replacing φιλεῖν, it becomes illegitimate to assign a whole series of subtle nuances to ἀγαπᾶν in the way that many have done:[32]

> Si un verbe devient très général, au point d'en remplacer deux ou trois autres, il est bien vain de lui prêter aussi et en même temps un sens très riche et très particulier.[33]

That is not to deny that ἀγαπᾶν could ever be used with a

---

[31] Examples taken from Joly, op. cit., pp. 38-40. Barclay (*Words*, p. 19) disputes the synonymity in Xen., but surely the reversal of verbs proves it.

[32] Joly, *Vocabulaire*, p. 36.   [33] Op. cit., p. 47.

special nuance; but once a word has become the current term for a particular idea, it is invalid to claim special reasons for its employment in a particular context. Rather, it must again be affirmed that it is the *context*, and not the prior history, which determines the nuance of a word in a specific case. Failure to perceive this results in "un véritable monstre linguistique", as Joly puts it in a very spirited passage.([34])

Granted this summary of the general picture outside the LXX, attention must now be given to the use of ἀγαπᾶν in the LXX itself.([35])

LXX USAGE

The study of LXX lexicography is both valuable and yet at the same time fraught with difficulty. It is impossible here to do more than allude to questions regarding the general character of LXX language, which have occasioned

---

([34]) Ibid. (See also his p. 8).
([35]) There is not space to examine in detail further evidence of ἀγαπᾶν taking on established senses of other words for 'love'; but three examples (culled from LSJ and BAGD) may be mentioned here. (1) ἀγαπᾶν + infin. 'be wont' is first attested in Arist. Oec. 1348ᵃ29; the sense is well established for φιλεῖν at least since Hdt. (LSJ φιλέω, II). (2) ἀγαπᾶν + infin., 'desire' is found in MAMA 1.176.1 (Laodicea Combusta, no date given), Anton.Lib. 40.1 (II A.D.); the same sense is found occasionally for στέργειν in Classical usage (Eurip. Ion 817) and also for ἐρᾶν (Soph. Ant. 220, cf. Hippocr. de Arte 7, etc.). (3) ἀγάπη + obj. gen. occurring in 2Th 2.10, 1Cl 55.5, closely parallels the similar use of φιλία (Pl. Rep 581a) and ἔρως (Aesch. Ag 540).

considerable work up to the present time.(36)
The fact that the LXX is for the most part a translation and not a Greek original raises inevitable questions about the naturalness of its Greek idiom; yet there is an inbuilt system of 'checks and balances' which should not be overlooked. For when a word such as ἀγαπᾶν is studied in the LXX, the reader is presented not merely with a single translator's choice of a translation equivalent but with the choice and non-choice of several different translators, working in different times, probably even different places and employing different techniques, whose usage and idiosyncrasies are likely to provide a check on one another.(37)

It is beyond the scope of the present paper to prove

---

(36) Cf., e.g., X. Jacques, "Le vocabulaire de la Septante - Vers une méthode de recherche et d'exposition", Bib 48 (1967) 296-301; C.Rabin, "The Translation process and character of the Septuagint", Textus 6 (1968) 1-26; S.P. Brock, "The phenomenon of the Septuagint", OTS 17 (1972) 11-36; E. Tov, "Studies in the vocabulary of the Septuagint - The relation between vocabulary and translation technique", Tarbiz 47 (1978) 120-38, I-II; S.P. Brock, "Aspects of translation technique in antiquity", GRBS 20 (1979) 69-87; J.A.L. Lee, A Lexical Study of the Septuagint Version of the Pentateuch [SBLSCS 14], (Chico, 1983).

(37) For questions of dating, provenance and translation technique, see, e.g. , H.B. Swete, An Introduction to the Old Testament in Greek (Cambridge, 1900), pp. 23ff.; S. Jellicoe, The Septuagint and Modern Study (Oxford, 1968), pp. 59-70; R.A. Kraft, "Septuagint", IDBSup, (1976), p.813; D. Barthélemy, Les devanciers d'Aquila (VTSup 10; 1963); Brock, "Phenomenon" (n. 36 above); H.M. Orlinsky, "The Septuagint as holy writ and the philosophy of the translators", HUCA 46 (1975) 89-114; Barr, Typology (n. 2 above). Joly's case would be strengthened had he taken into account these factors.

which parts of the LXX have been translated into idiomatic Greek: that has been sufficiently shown by others.(³⁸) However, the fact that אהב and derivatives are not always translated by ἀγαπᾶν and derivatives (and conversely that ἀγαπᾶν and derivatives do not always stand for some form of the root אהב) shows that ἀγαπᾶν -- common throughout the LXX -- has not been used in a merely mechanical way. That provides sufficient incentive to continue the present study! Nonetheless, caution will be necessary if conclusions are to be drawn from any of the more mechanically translated sections of the LXX.(³⁹)

Given constraints of space, ἀγαπᾶν will be studied here -- along with other vocabulary for 'love' -- in three sections of the LXX only: the Pentateuch, Isaiah and Proverbs. Each is considered, on independent criteria, to have at least reasonable regard for normal Greek usage.(⁴⁰)

(³⁸) See, e.g., H.St.J. Thackeray, *A Grammar of the Old Testament in Greek* (Cambridge, 1900), p. 13; Kraft, "Septuagint", 813f.; Barr, *Typology*, pp. 6-9; E. Tov, *The Textcritical use of the Septuagint in Biblical Research* (Jerusalem, 1981), pp. 54-59, 63.
(³⁹) On this question. cf. E. Tov, "Three Dimensions of LXX Words", *RB* 83 (1976) 529-44; J.A.L. Lee, "Equivocal and stereotyped renderings in the LXX', *RB* 87 (1980) 104-17; Tov, *Text-Critical*, pp. 50-66.
(⁴⁰) Thackeray, *Grammar*, p. 13; Kraft, "Septuagint", p. 814.

THE PENTATEUCH

In the Pentateuch, ἀγαπᾶν occurs some forty-one times, and is almost the only word for 'love'. It is generally used as the equivalent of the Hebrew אהב, and consequently has a wide range of application. It describes the various family relations: parents' love for children (Ge 22.2 +); a husband's love for his wife (Ge 24.67 +). It is used of a man's love for a woman (Ge 29.18ff.; 34.3); and of 'love' in social relationships (servant for master, De 15.16; Ex 21.5; man for neighbour (τὸν πλησίον σου), Le 19.18, and for strangers([41]) (ὁ προσήλυτος ὁ προσπορευόμενος πρὸς ἡμᾶς), ibid. v. 34). These senses are all natural outside the LXX, and the translator may be felt to be following idiomatic Greek usage.

In particular, however, the word is also used of 'love' in a religious context. Following the Hebrew, it occurs once in Exodus (20.6), and twenty-one times in Deuteronomy (including ἠγαπημένος below). Used of God's love for His people (De 4.37+) and for the stranger (ibid. 10.18), parallels may be drawn from outside usage:([42]) but

---

([41]) See Lee ("Equivocal and stereotyped renderings", 112-13, n. 27) for this meaning of προσήλυτος. [A further discussion on this question may be found in T. Muraoka, "Towards a Septuagint lexicon" in C.E. Cox (ed.), *VI Congress of the International Organization for Septuagint and Cognate Studies: Jerusalem 1986* [SBLSCS 23] (Atlanta, 1987), pp. 255-76. - Ed.]

([42]) e.g. ἠγαπημένος ὑπὸ τοῦ Θεᾶ in the Rosetta Stone (*OGI* 90.4,8,9,37,49; II B.C.) and ἠγαπημένος ὑπὸ τῆς Ἴσιδος Wilcken, *Chrest.*, I.109.12; III B.C.).

in the sense of the people's love for God (Ex 20.6; De 5.10 +), a sense which continues in later usage: LSJ suggest that it is first attested here, and BAGD only gives one example from a (later) pagan source.([43])

ἠγαπημένος is used for (יהוה) ידיד, of Benjamin, in De 32.12. It is also the rendering that is given for the name ישרון in all three of its occurrences in Deuteronomy (32.15; 33.5,26): this may be exegetical.([44])

The adjective ἀγαπητός occurs in Ge 22.2,12,16 of an 'only' son:

v. 2: Λαβὲ τὸν υἱόν σου τὸν ἀγαπητόν
     MT: קח־נא את־בנך את־יחידך.

This is in accordance with an established use.([45])

Generally, therefore, the use of ἀγαπᾶν and derivatives in the Pentateuch appears to be fairly idiomatic Greek. An exception may possibly be felt with the rather literal *syntax* of παρὰ τὸ ἀγαπᾶν αὐτὸν αὐτήν in Ge 29.20 (MT באהבתו אתה), where it may be felt that a noun could have been better: but note that neither ἀγάπησις nor ἀγάπη -- nor yet אהבה as a noun -- occurs in the Pentateuch.

This assessment is supported by the use of the verb φιλεῖν.

Φιλεῖν is generally used for נשק (Qal and Pi'el), with

([43]) Dio Chrys. 12.61 (A.D. 97).
([44]) (Also at Is 44.2). The Targum renders as ישראל: is this connected with the (explanatory?) double rendering at De 32.15? οἱ γ', however, render etymologically (εὐθύς).
([45]) Hom. *Od.* 2.365 +; Hesychius: ἀγαπητός· μονογενής.

'Αγαπᾶν in the LXX   65

its common meaning 'kiss': (so, always, καταφιλεῖν).(⁴⁶)
There are, however, four cases where it means 'love'.
In Genesis 27, φιλεῖν is used three times (vv. 4,9,14
for אהב, with the object 'food' (ἐδέσματα).(⁴⁷)
The other occurrence is in Ge 37.4, which deserves
closer attention. Vv 3,4 read as follows:

Ιακωβ δὲ ἠγάπα τὸν Ιωσηφ παρὰ πάντας τοὺς υἱοὺς αὐτοῦ,
ὅτι υἱὸς γήρους ἦν αὐτῷ· ἐποίησεν δὲ αὐτῷ χιτῶνα
ποικίλον. ἰδόντες δὲ οἱ ἀδελφοὶ αὐτοῦ ὅτι αὐτὸν ὁ

πατὴρ φιλεῖ ἐκ τῶν Ιακωβ δὲ ἠγάπα τὸν Ιωσηφ παρὰ
πάντας τοὺς υἱοὺς αὐτοῦ, ὅτι υἱὸς γήρους ἦν αὐτῷ·
ἐποίησεν δὲ αὐτῷ χιτῶνα ποικίλον. ἰδόντες δὲ οἱ ἀδελφοὶ αὐτοῦ ὅτι αὐτὸν ὁ πατὴρ φιλεῖ ἐκ τῶν υἱῶν αὐτοῦ,
ἐμίσησαν αὐτὸν καὶ οὐκ ἐδύναντο λαλεῖν αὐτῷ οὐδὲν
εἰρηνικόν.

What is interesting here is that the same Hebrew word
(אהב) is rendered in the one case by ἀγαπᾶν, in the other
by φιλεῖν, and both are being used in the context of
Jacob's love for his son Joseph. The question naturally
arises whether there is any significance in the variation.
C.F. Hogg argues that there is:

> To me... the change from ἀγαπάω to φιλέω suggests a
> nice discrimination on the part of the translators,

(⁴⁶) καταφιλεῖν is the only compound of φιλεῖν in the LXX
(14 times; always for נשק except 3Ki 2.19 [MT וישתחו לה
did the translators read a form of נשק?]).
(⁴⁷) LSJ (φιλέω, 5) cite it with the object Πράμνιον
οἶνον, Ephiph. 28 (IV B.C.). Was ἀγαπᾶν used of food? LSJ
attest the noun ἀγάπημα, 'dainty dish' (Axioxic. 4.6 [IV
B.C.]), but this may prove nothing.

rather than establishes an equality between the words. Jacob loved Joseph with a discerning love based upon his knowledge of the lad's character, and perhaps because he anticipated for him a peculiar place in the development of the Divine purposes, whereas the brethren could only perceive an inordinate affection in their father's treatment of his younger son.[48]

However, his argument is less than convincing; for whilst the Pentateuch itself affords no parallel for this variation, both verbs are naturally used of parents' love for their children; and the form of the Hebrew here provides no support for the subtlety suggested.[49] (If Hogg were correct, it might well be asked why φιλεῖν was not more frequently used in the LXX in purely domestic or social contexts.) Rather, the true explanation seems to be that the variation is purely stylistic: notice that v. 4 contains the word pair φιλεῖν - μισεῖν, which has already been mentioned as enjoying some favour in Classical and post-Classical Greek.[50] There is no reason to suppose that the variation of verbs drew the special gaze of the original readers.

---

[48] C.F. Hogg, "Note on ἀγαπάω and φιλέω," *ExpTim* 38 (1927) 379f.
[49] A couple of trivial variations between LXX and MT in v. 4 do not affect this.
[50] Joly (*Vocabulaire*, p. 51) mentions this passage, but fails to observe the φιλεῖν - μισεῖν pair; hence his n. 8 on p. 38 needs correction.

No other words for 'love' are used in the Pentateuch.(⁵¹)

ISAIAH

In Isaiah, ἀγαπᾶν is again the usual word for 'love'.(⁵²) The adjective ἀγαπητός occurs twice, both times in the sense 'beloved'. (⁵³) The verb is used of God's love for Abraham (41.8; 51.2)(⁵⁴) and His people in general (43.4; 48.14; 60.10; 63.9);(⁵⁵) also of the proselyte's love for God (56.6). It is used of love for a son in 3.25.(⁵⁶)

(⁵¹) Apart from ἀποστέρξεις (A ἀποστρέψεις), 'love no more' ('rid of love', LSJ), De 15.7 (obj. τὴν καρδίαν σου). This is the only occurrence of a form of στέργειν outside the Apocrypha.

(⁵²) Usually for אהב; but 60.10 for רחם (Pi.); ἠγαπημένος for ידיד (5.1 twice), שעשועים (5.7) and ישרון (44.2, ἠγαπημένος Ισραηλ double rendering: see n. 44 above).

(⁵³) 5.1 (for דוד: only there in the whole LXX; but used by Symmachus in Song of Solomon [see E. Hatch & H.A. Redpath, *A Concordance to the Septuagint* (Oxford, 1897) 1.7]); and 26.17 (no equivalent in MT). Mt 12.18 (Is 42.1) is not quoted from LXX.

(⁵⁴) Both cases are interesting as they differ from MT. 41.8 MT reads זרע אברהם אהבי. 51.2 involves a double rendering: the sense in LXX is clear, but 'love' is not in MT; perhaps some confusion between ר and ה in the *Vorlage* (cf. 6.11 [תשאה] and 8.12 [קשר]?) has produced conflation of forms based on וארבהו and ואהבהו respectively: if so, the reading in B may indicate non-conflation rather than haplography (cf. edd.crit.); haplography by the MT is less likely given the progression of the verbs.

(⁵⁵) 63:9 reads διὰ τὸ ἀγαπᾶν αὐτούς for בְּאַהֲבָתוֹ (noun: cf. ובחמלתו following; but ἀγάπησις and ἀγάπη are not used in Isaiah). This verse in LXX differs considerably from MT.

(⁵⁶) Relation of LXX to MT is problematic here, but sense of LXX is *very* clear.

Beyond what the Pentateuch offers, however, ἀγαπᾶν also occurs in the following contexts. In 57.8, in an extended metaphor, it is used of the illicit love of the nation for its sexual partners: ἠγάπησας τοὺς κοιμωμένους μετὰ σοῦ.([57]) It is also used with impersonal objects: God's love for justice (61.8, in opposition to μισῶν ἁρπάγματα ἐξ ἀδικίας); the rulers' eagerness for bribes (δῶρα, 1.23); and, in a religious context, of love for Jerusalem (66.10).([58]) The only other occurrence of a verb for 'love' in Isaiah is φιλεῖν with the infinitive, 'like to... ', in 56.10. The passage consists of a description of the people of the city -- the MT specifies the watchmen but this detail is omitted in the LXX -- under the metaphor of lazy dogs:

πάντες κύνες ἐνεοί, οὐ δυνήσονται ὑλακτεῖν, ἐνυπνια-
ζόμενοι κοίτην, φιλοῦντες νυστάξαι.
MT: ... אהבי לנום

This sense of φιλεῖν is common; and it is virtually synonymous with ἀγαπᾶν with the infinitive, except that the latter appears only to be used with human subjects, whereas φιλεῖν is of much wider application.([59])

From this it can be seen that the use of ἀγαπᾶν for אהב in Isaiah is not merely mechanical, and we may reasonably infer that attention is being given to natural Greek usage.([60])

([57]) The object is מִשְׁכָּבָם in MT. LXX has prob. suffered haplography of a few words through homoeoteleuton in the Hebrew (... הרחבת ... מהם אהבת).
([58]) For some reason this has become corrupted in A, S^c and C, which all read compounds of οἰκεῖν.
([59]) Cf. LSJ, φιλέω, II.2. Both also mean 'be wont'.
([60]) Cf. Thackeray (Grammar, p. 13) : "Good κοινή".

PROVERBS

The Book of Proverbs is probably the most illustrative of the later books of the LXX in its use of Greek words for 'love'. One reason for this is that the translation is quite free, even paraphrastic; and another reason is the relatively large number of examples that are offered. Like the Books of Job and Esther, it is written in a literary style;([61]) but for that reason it at times gives insight into the contemporary usage of ἀγαπᾶν and its derivatives.

The verb ἀγαπᾶν occurs quite frequently, usually as a translation of אהב, but also for רחם (Pu.) (28.13), קנה (לב) (15.32) and שמר (תורה) (28.4).([62]) In line with the contents of the Book, it is used of God's love for men, also of people's love for teaching, instruction, virtues, etc. In 20.13 it is followed by the infinitive and means 'to be fond of', 'make a habit of':

μὴ ἀγάπα καταλαλεῖν, ἵνα μὴ ἐξαρθῇς

This sense has already been noted as idiomatic Greek.([63])

In 30.15, ἀγαπήσει ἀγαπώμεναι is written for the difficult הב הב of the MT, describing the three (sic)

([61]) S. Jellicoe (*Septuagint and Modern Study*, p. 68) calls it "the work of a classical scholar who put much of his work into iambics and hexameters."

([62]) 28.17a is probably an inner-Greek corruption.

([63]) Note that the MT (... שְׁנָה אַל־תֶּאֱהַב) is rather different; so this is a good example of the Greek use. In 22.14a (not in MT), ἀγαπᾶν + infin. means 'wish to' (cf. Ps 33.13 and n. 35 (2) above).

daughters of the βδέλλη.(⁶⁴) ἀγαπώμενος also occurs in 4.3, of the 'dear' son (or even 'only son': ἀγαπητός is not used in Proverbs, though this may not be of importance).

The comparative frequency of the verbs ἀγαπᾶν, φιλεῖν, and ἐρᾶν in Proverbs is interesting. As has been indicated, ἀγαπᾶν is the most frequent; ἐρᾶν occurs once (4.6), and in fact only twice more in the whole LXX (Est 2.17, and the apocryphal 1Es 4.24); φιλεῖν occurs five times, in two of those instances with the meaning 'kiss' (7.13; 24.26).

In 8.17 we read, ἐγὼ τοὺς ἐμέ φιλοῦντας ἀγαπῶ (MT אֲנִי אֹהֲבֶיהָ אֵהָב -- the speaker is Wisdom personified). Here, τοὺς ἐμὲ φιλοῦντας probably simply means 'my friends',(⁶⁵) the same as φίλοι (14.20) and φίλου (27.6), both for the Qal participle of אהב, and τοῖς ἐμὲ ἀγαπῶσιν in 8.21. These variations can only exist for literary effect.

The use of ἐρᾶν for love of wisdom (in 4.6) implies 'passionate desire':

ἐράσθητι αὐτῆς, καὶ τηρήσει σε.
This is free elaboration on the part of the translator -- the Hebrew simply reads אֱהָבֶהָ -- but it is quite in keeping with the context. ἐρᾶν properly denotes sexual love, but it is by no means always so used. It is used, for instance, of τυραννίς by Archilochus (25.3; VII B.C.);

(⁶⁴) The translator is clearly struggling to make sense of the context. I find it unnecessary to posit with Fichtner (BHS) that he read שׁלשׁ: rather, he is influenced by αἱ τρεῖς αὗται in the next clause. On הב הב, cf. יְהָבְךָ at Ps 54.23 (LXX τὴν μέριμνάν σου, but Aquila, Symmachus and Quinta ἀγαπήσει σε [= יֶחְבְּךָ?]) and LXX/MT at Ho 8.12,13.
(⁶⁵) Freq. in papyri. Cf. also Je 22.22.

BAGD cites a place in Philo where the object is ἀληθείας (*Spec.Leg.* 2.258).

Granted the explanation of 8.21 above, ἀγαπᾶν is not used in Proverbs of love for 'wisdom'. In 29.3, however, φιλεῖν is so used: ἀνδρὸς φιλοῦντος (אֹהֵב) σοφίαν εὐφραίνεται πατὴρ αὐτοῦ.

The distinction may be purely coincidental; or it may reflect the translator's literary background: note, for instance, the evidence in Greek of the compound words φιλοσοφεῖν and φιλοσοφία.[66]

In 21.17, ἀγαπᾶν and φιλεῖν are used once each for the MT אהב:

ἀνὴρ ἐνδεὴς ἀγαπᾷ εὐφροσύνην
φιλῶν οἶνον καὶ ἔλαιον εἰς πλοῦτον.

This may be merely for the sake of literary variation, but one cannot help noting that ἀγαπᾶν is used with the abstract noun εὐφροσύνη, whilst φιλεῖν is being used of fondness for *food* -- a sense already noted in the Pentateuch.[67]

The Greek noun ἀγάπη is not used at all in this Book. Instead, φιλία occurs nine or ten times, five of those instances standing for אהבה. Outside Proverbs, φιλία is used only in the Apocrypha (where, however, it is fairly common, occurring in Wisdom, Ecclesiasticus and Maccabees). It is used, therefore, both of friendship (or love) in general (10.12; 15.17; 17.9; 19.7; 25.10a [not in MT]; 27.5) and also of erotic love both within (5.19) and

---

[66] φιλοσοφεῖν/-ία in LXX in 4Maccabees; φιλόσοφος in Daniel LXX and 4Maccabees. The existence of these words, of course, proves little: ἀγαπ- forms no compounds, but compounds in φιλ(ο)- are normal.
[67] Cf. at n. 47 above.

without (7.18) marriage. The impression gained is that the translator has avoided the (presumably) more recent word ἀγάπη for literary reasons. Suffice it to note that Symmachus -- and naturally Aquila and Theodotion -- employs ἀγάπη in his translation of Proverbs.(68)

It is worth noting, finally, that the noun ἔρως is used twice in Proverbs -- only here in the whole LXX. In 7.18 it is used of erotic love, for אֲהָבִים (hapax), parallel to φιλία.(69) In 30.16, ἔρως γυναικός is listed as one of the things which is never satisfied (οὐκ ἠρκέσθη εἰπεῖν 'Ικανόν, v. 15):(70) the construction with an objective genitive is known from Classical times.(71)

CONCLUSIONS

Even in the more idiomatic sections of the LXX, ἀγαπᾶν is far more common than any of its synonyms. Given the differing translation techniques and styles encountered in the LXX, very strong evidence is presented that it was becoming (or had already become) the ordinary word for 'love' in Koine Greek.

It is clearly to be expected that if ἀγαπᾶν was becoming the regular word for 'love', then other words would be disappearing or declining. Here, again, the LXX

---

(68) Hatch & Redpath (*Concordance*, I.7) cite 10.12 for Aquila and Symmachus, 15.17 for Aquila, Symmachus and Theodotion, and 7.18 for Aquila and Theodotion.

(69) For φιλεῖν with ἐρᾶν, see LSJ, φιλέω, I.3.

(70) The sense of the Greek is clear, but its relation to the Hebrew is problematical. ἔρως may perhaps come from a corruption of עצר transliterated into Greek characters, but the translator of Proverbs is not known for the use of transliteration (Thackeray, *Grammar*, p. 32).

(71) LSJ cite Soph. *Tr.* 433; Eurip. *Ion* 67.

provides strong witness -- drawn from different translators, different localities(?) and dates -- that ἀγαπᾶν had all but replaced φιλεῖν as the ordinary word for 'love' in Koine.

This evidence complements and is corroborated by what was seen of its external Greek use earlier in this paper. Interestingly, it illustrates the value of the LXX as a tool for the study of Greek lexicography, provided that the special techniques of the translators are kept in mind. In the case of the terms under consideration here, further documentation is provided of the change taking place within the Greek language; this is all the more striking because of the prominence of the vocabulary of 'love' in the OT when viewed against its sporadic occurrence in the papyri and contemporary literature.

The partial survival of φιλεῖν has been noted, either as a literary variation from ἀγαπᾶν or as a survivor in traditional collocations such as the word pair φιλεῖν - μισεῖν. However, the use of ἀγαπᾶν as an established alternative to φιλεῖν in the pair has been seen in external literature and receives further attestation in the LXX: (it is commonly used as the antonym of μισεῖν in the Pentateuch, which may be presumed to be following accepted idiom; but still more indicative is its occurrence in Pr 8.36, οἱ μισοῦντές με ἀγαπῶσιν θάνατον, the translator of which is noted for his literary predilections).

The LXX is known to be a witness to some so-called 'hibernations' within the Greek language. These are words or meanings which may be presumed to have been part of the vernacular language but which are not as yet attested outside the LXX.[72] From the word-group treated in the

---

[72] Cf. Lee, *Lexical Study*, p. 52, n. 29.

present study there comes a striking example in the noun ἀγάπη (not actually discussed above), whose first certain occurrence in extant Greek literature is at LXX Je 2.2 (used there of love between God and man portrayed under the figure of τελείωσις 'marriage'). Apart from the lack of prior external attestation, there are no grounds for supposing that ἀγάπη was anything other than a common Greek word in the translators' day. It is a natural formation from its stem; and in view of the 'shaky' literary history of ἀγάπησις, which does not appear to have survived long in popular use (see the lexica), its currency is most likely. This supposition is supported by the fact that when ἀγάπη does appear -- within and beyond the LXX -- it is used with the same range of application as the verb ἀγαπᾶν. What is likely, however, is that ἀγάπη had only recently developed within Koine, as it seems consciously to have been avoided by the literary translator of Proverbs; a new formation is generally used long in popular speech before it is received into literary usage.([73])

([73]) Joly (*Vocabulaire*, p. 48) suggests that Egypt may have been marginally ahead of other Greek-speaking regions in the shift towards the predominance of ἀγαπᾶν; he notes that στέργειν and ἐρᾶν were still reasonably popular in pagan literature though scarcely attested in LXX. His conclusion may or may not be necessary: LXX language may reflect the vernacular more closely than the pagan writers do. A. Ceresa-Gastaldo ("ΑΓΑΠΗ nei documenti estranei all'influsso biblico", *Rivista di Filologia* NS 31 [1953] 394) notes the reconstruction of ἀγάπη in a sepulchral inscription of 27 B.C.; it occurs clearly in a pagan inscription of the third century A.D., *Supplementum Epigraphicum Graecum* 8 (1937) 11.6: ... ἥ τίς ὑπὸ πάτρης τόσσην ἔσχ' ἀγάπην;

The later books of the LXX have not been able to be studied in detail here, particularly Ezra-Nehemiah, Ecclesiastes and the books of the *kaige* recension, which give some indication of a fixed use of ἀγαπᾶν as a stereotyped equivalent for the Hebrew אהב (though not without exception, attributable sometimes to the survival of features of an unrevised text). This comes from their concern for more formal correspondence between elements of the Hebrew and Greek texts than is found in the earlier and in the more literary books.([74]) Where this has happened, it is clearly invalid to isolate the senses in which ἀγαπᾶν / ἀγάπη appear to be being used; however, the very fact that ἀγάπη may be used as a stereotype (see lexical entry below) implies that it was already known in everyday Greek, since its attestation in the LXX is otherwise less strong than that of ἀγάπησις.

In the light of the foregoing, it will be seen that it is illegitimate to draw theological conclusions about the LXX translators' choice of ἀγαπᾶν as a translation equivalent for the Hebrew אהב. The great frequency with which ἀγαπᾶν is used in the LXX in a *religious* sense is attributable solely to the frequency of that idea in the Hebrew.([75]) Even its use as applied to man's love for God is unlikely to be a sense developed specifically by the LXX translators, even despite its lack of earlier pagan attestation. In all probability, it was the natural word to use when speaking of love for God in Koine Greek, but

---

([74]) See Brock, "Aspects" (n. 36 above), 75-79; Barr, *Typology*, pp. 36f.
([75]) ἀγάπη 'alms', 'charity' is attested in IV/V A.D. (*P.Gen.* 14); but that is a development far removed from its use in LXX.

certain cultures might in practice not express that idea very commonly. What is likely, then, is that the *meaning* was natural, but that the *idea* received specific development within Judaism and Christianity. The use of the verb in a speech of the pagan writer Dio Chrysostom (A.D. 97) strongly supports this conclusion.[76]

In conclusion, the remarkable frequency with which ἀγαπᾶν is used in the LXX is due finally to one reason alone -- that at the time when the LXX was translated **it was the ordinary Greek word for 'love'** and so was capable of translating אהב in almost every instance where the latter occurred in the OT. Any developments in the use of ἀγαπᾶν across the LXX, such as its possible employment as a stereotyped equivalent of אהב in later books, are founded on this sole starting-point. Accordingly, the capacity which ἀγαπᾶν possessed for conveying theological truth -- whether or not this directly interested the LXX translators themselves -- lay in the fact that **as a living word in common use it could be moulded by the** *context* **to convey the appropriate level of meaning.** Any arguments, therefore, about its inherent suitability based on its history four or five centuries before are seen to be irrelevant. It is hoped that exegesis of the LXX and NT will bear these conclusions in mind.

---

[76] 12.32: ἐπινοοῦντες οὐκ ἐδύναντο μὴ θαυμάζειν καὶ ἀγαπᾶν τὸ δαιμόνιον. 12.61: ἀτεχνῶς γὰρ ὥσπερ νήπιοι παῖδες πατρὸς ἢ μητρὸς ἀπεσπασμένοι δεινὸν ἵμερον ἔχοντες καὶ πόθον ὀρέγουσι χεῖρας οὐ παροῦσι πολλάκις ὀνειρώττοντες, οὕτω καὶ θεοῖς ἄνθρωποι ἀγαπῶντες δικαίως διά τε εὐεργεσίαν καὶ συγγένειαν προθυμούμενοι πάντα τρόπον συνεῖναί τε καὶ ὁμιλεῖν.

'Αγαπᾶν in the LXX

LEXICAL ENTRIES

The pages which follow contain suggested lexical entries for ἀγαπάω, ἀγάπησις, ἀγάπη, and ἀγαπητός in the LXX, including their uses in the books which have not been discussed above.

ἀγαπάω

I. *love, be fond of*:
1. of social relations:
   a. domestic: parent - child (Ge 22.2 +) and vice versa (Ru 4.15); husband - wife (Ge 24.67 +; opp. μισεῖν, De 21.15-17); man - woman (Ge 29.18ff.;34.3 +); servant - master (De 15.16; Ex 21.5). Involving preference: ἀγαπᾶν τινα μᾶλλον ἤ τινα (Ge 29.30), παρά τινι (Ge 37.3), ὑπέρ τινα (1Kg 1.5; 2Ch 11.21).
   b. social: for neighbour, τὸν πλησίον σου, Le 19.18; for strangers, ὁ προσήλυτος ὁ προσπορευόμενος πρὸς ἡμᾶς Le 19.34.
   c. Wisdom for her friends: Pr 8.17 ἐγὼ τοὺς ἐμὲ φιλοῦντας ἀγαπῶ.
   d. οἱ ἀγαπῶντές τινα = *one's friends*, Pr 8.21 (cf. sim. οἱ φιλοῦντές τινα, 8.17); (La 1.2).
   e. in formal context, *regard, esteem, delight in*: Est 6.9 ὃν ὁ βασιλεὺς ἀγαπᾷ (MT אשר המלך חפץ ביקרו).
2. religious
   a. God for His people: De 4.37 +; for Abraham, Is 41.8; 51.2.
   b. God for the stranger: De 10.18.
   c. man for God: Ex 20.6; De 5.10 +; (a sense apparently first attested in the LXX, but not unnatural as Greek: cf. Dio Chrysostom 12.32, 61 [A.D. 97]).
   d. God's people for Jerusalem: Is 66.10 (not A S[c] C).
   e. man for idols: Jer 8.2.

3. erotic: Ho 3.1; Is 57.8 (metaph.) ἠγάπησας τοὺς κοιμωμένους μετὰ σοῦ.

4. to show love, ? Ho 2.25 B V (var. ἐλεήσω). Ps 93.19 κύριε, κατὰ τὸ πλῆθος τῶν ὀδυνῶν μου ἐν τῇ καρδίᾳ μου αἱ παρακλήσεις σου ἠγάπησαν τὴν ψυχήν μου.

5. pf. pass. ptcpl. ἠγαπημένος, dear, beloved:

a. in general, 2Ki 1.23 (// ὡραῖοι).

b. of God's 'beloved' people, Je 11.15 +; ἠγαπημένος ὑπὸ κυρίου, De 33.12 (Benjamin); cf. τὴν οὐκ ἠγαπημένην Ho 2.25 B V. ὁ ἠγαπημένος as a rendering of יְשֻׁרוּן (of Israel) at De 32.15; 33.5,26; Is 44.2, is prob. exegetical. (Cf. Ps 28.6 28.6 [MT וִישֻׁרָיו]).

c. of the θυσιαστήρια which God esteemed, Ho 8.11,12.

II. of impersonal objects, love, desire:

1. δικαιοσύνην, Is 61.8 (opp. μισῶν ἁρπάγματα ἐξ ἀδικίας), 1Ch 29.17 (MT רצה); εὐφροσύνην, Pr 21.17; θάνατον, Pr 8.36 (opp. μισοῦντές με [Wisdom]); δῶρα (bribes), Is 1.23; πονηρὰ καὶ μοιχαλίν (of a prostitute), Ho 3.1.

2. ἀγαπᾶν τι ὑπέρ τι = prefer (cf. I.1.a.): Ct 1.4 ἀγαπήσομεν μαστούς σου ὑπὲρ οἶνον.

3. restrictive sense, be content with, accept: Poss. sense at Je 5.31 ... καὶ ὁ λαός μου ἠγάπησεν οὕτως; Da 4.27 LXX τούτους τοὺς λόγους ἀγάπησον; cf. Pr 28.4 οὕτως οἱ ἐγκαταλείποντες τὸν νόμον ἐγκωμιάζουσιν ἀσέβειαν, οἱ δὲ ἀγαπῶντες τὸν νόμον περιβάλλουσιν ἑαυτοῖς τεῖχος. (Doubtfully the sense at Ps 114.1 [absol.], where prob. stereotype for Heb. אהב.)

III. with infin.:

1. be fond of, make a habit of, Pr 20.13 μὴ ἀγάπα καταλαλεῖν.

2. wish to, Ps 33.13 ἀγαπῶν ἡμέρας ἰδεῖν ἀγαθάς (syntax diverges from MT).

IV. with infin.: be wont to: poss. sense at Je 14.10

ἠγάπησαν κινεῖν πόδας αὐτῶν; Ho 12.8 Χανααν ἐν χειρὶ ζυγὸς ἀδικίας, καταδυναστεύειν ἠγάπησε.

Of all the verbs for love in the Greek Bible, ἀγαπάω is by far the most common. In some books (e.g. Ezra-Nehemiah, Ecclesiastes and the books of the kaige recension), it may be employed as a stereotyped equivalent of the Heb. אהב, but certainty is impossible because the resultant Greek is seldom difficult.

ἀγάπησις, affection, love
(The meaning love, not given in LSJ, is evident at Je 2.33)

a. human: 2Ki 1.26 (bis) ἐθαυμαστώθη ἡ ἀγάπησίς (O-A ἀγάπη) σου ἐμοὶ ὑπὲρ ἀγάπησιν (O† ἀγάπην) γυναικῶν; Ps 108. 5 (opp. μῖσος); erotic, Je 2.33 (metaph.).
b. of God for man: Je 38.3 'Αγάπησιν αἰωνίαν ἠγάπησά σε; Ho 11.4; Hb 3.4; Ze 3.17 καινιεῖ σε ἐν τῇ ἀγαπήσει (S* † εὐφροσύνῃ) αὐτοῦ.
c. of man for God (?): Si 48.11 μακάριοι οἱ ἐν ἀγαπήσει (S* † ἀγάπῃ) κεκοιμημένοι.
d. for wisdom: Si 40.20.
e. of the leech for its young: Pr 30.15 τῇ βδέλλῃ τρεῖς [sic] θυγατέρες ἦσαν ἀγαπήσει ἀγαπώμεναι (MT שׁתֵּי ...הב הב בָּנוֹת הַב הַב).

Related words: ἀγάπη, ἔρως, στοργή, φιλία. There is evidence of a shift of preference over time from ἀγάπησις to ἀγάπη (cf. variant readings at 2Ki 1.26(O) and Si 48. 11(S*). Despite the limited data offered in the LXX, it may be observed that ἀγάπησις is preferred to ἀγάπη in the earlier and in the more literary translation units. [All reff. cited.]

ἀγάπη, *love*.

A.a. of man for God: Je 2.2 καὶ εἶπεν Τάδε λέγει κύριος Ἐμνήσθην ἐλέους νεότητός σου καὶ ἀγάπης τελειώσεώς σου.
b. of God for man: Wi 3.9 οἱ πιστοὶ ἐν ἀγάπῃ προσμενοῦσιν αὐτῷ.
c. for wisdom: Wi 6.17,18.
d. human love: cf. B. below.
B. Most occurrences of ἀγάπη are found in books of the *kaige* recension and in Ecclesiastes, where the choice of translation may be merely as a stereotyped equivalent for the Hebrew word אהבה: cf. ἀγαπᾶν very freq. for אהב):
a. opp. μῖσος: 2Ki 13.15 ὅτι μέγα τὸ μῖσος, ὃ ἐμίσησεν αὐτήν, ὑπὲρ τὴν ἀγάπην, ἣν ἠγάπησεν αὐτήν; Ec 9.1,6.
b. *passim* in Song of Solomon: 2.4; 2:5 (τετρωμένη ἀγάπης ἐγώ, sim. 5.8); 2.7 (ἐὰν ἐγείρητε καὶ ἐξεγείρητε τὴν ἀγάπην, sim. 3.5; cf. 8.4); 3.10; 8.6 (κραταιὰ ὡς θάνατος ἀγάπη); 8.7 (*bis*); 7.7 as vocative, τί ὡραιώθης καὶ τί ἡδύνθης, ἀγάπη, ἐν τρυφαῖς σου; Only twice, however, is the resultant Greek awkward (Ct 2.4; 3.10).
C. Variant reading for ἀγάπησις at 2Ki 1.26(O) and Si 48.11(S*).

Jer 2.2 is the first certain documented use of this word in extant Greek literature. However, its apparent use as a stereotyped translation in B. above can be satisfactorily explained only on the basis that it was already established in contemporary Greek idiom, since its background in the LXX itself is not strong; otherwise ἀγάπησις could conceivably have been used.

Related words: ἀγάπησις (q.v.), ἔρως, στροργή, φιλία.
[All reff. cited.]

ἀγαπητός

I. 1. of things, *desirable, pleasant, loved*: σκηνώματα [κυρίου], Ps 83.2; βδέλυγμα, Si 15.13; prob. also the sense at Za 13.6 ἐν τῷ οἴκῳ τῷ ἀγαπητῷ μου.

2. an *only* child: son, Ge 22.2,12,16; mourning over the death of an only son: Je 6.26; Am 8.10; Za 12.10; daughter, Jdg 11.34A καὶ αὕτη μονογενὴς αὐτῷ ἀγαπητή; To 3.10S.

3. of persons, *beloved*:

a. in general, To 10.13; Bar 4.16; Sus 63 LXX; prob. also Je 38.20 υἱὸς ἀγαπητὸς Εφραιμ ἐμοί, παιδίον ἐντρυφῶν (unless this should be classified under 2. above).

b. plur., of God's people, οἱ ἀγαπητοὶ αὐτοῦ / σου: Ps 59.7 (// Ps 107.7); Ps 126.2.

c. specifically, ὁ ἀγαπητός = the (Messianic) king: Is 5.1; 26:17; Ps 44 *tit*. (For Ps 67.13, see II. below.)

II. Indeterminable sense at Ps 67.13 ὁ βασιλεὺς τῶν δυνάμεων τοῦ ἀγαπητοῦ (BO + τοῦ ἀγαπητοῦ) (MT מַלְכֵי־ צְבָאוֹת יִדֹּדוּן יִדֹּדוּן). Perhaps classify under I.3.c. above; but since ἀγαπητός is used as the standard equivalent of יָדִיד (5x) in the Psalms, the rendering here may be simply mechanical.

[All reff. cited.]

"Greek Words and Hebrew Meanings"

Emanuel Tov

Greek Words and Hebrew Meanings - Studies in the Semantics of Soteriological Terms , SNTS Monograph Series 5 (Cambridge, 1967) is the name of an important work by D. Hill. It shows that certain words are used in the NT in senses which reflect their Hebraic background (through the LXX) rather than their Greek heritage. In the wake of that book the following analysis centers on a few words which carry some senses which have been determined by the Hebrew. The analysis is not limited to these problems related to the Hebrew background of the words or senses; rather it treats the lexicographical description of these words in full. At the end of each analysis a sample entry for a LXX lexicon is suggested.

1. δικαίωμα

Under the relevant entry in LSJ, we note the following description:

act of right, opp. ἀδίκημα, Arist.; *duty*, Philo 2.199; prop. *amendment of a wrong*, opp. δικαιοπράγημα, Aristotle; hence:

I a. *judgement, penalty*, Plato
  b. *justification, plea of right*, Thucydides I 41,1, Isocrates, Aristotle, LXX 2Ki 19.28(29), PLond ii AD

c. pl. *pleadings, documents in a suit*, papyri iii B.C., also *credentials* pap ii A.D.
d. *act of* δικαίωσις i 3, N.T.

II *ordinance, decree*, LXX Ge 26.5 Ex 15.26 (pl.), al., NT

The lexicon of Liddell, Scott, and Jones thus describes in section I the basic meaning of δικαίωμα as a legal term, a term connected with the world of lawsuits. At the same time, in II it provides the meaning "ordinance, decree" for the LXX and literature depending on it.

The first question which comes to mind is whether the LXX also reflects some of the *basic* meanings of the word such as those recorded outside the LXX.

[I] LSJ records one occurrence of the meaning "justification" for the LXX. In the *ThDNT* this sense is defined as "legal ground or claim". The example provided is:

2Ki 19.29 καὶ τί ἐστίν μοι ἔτι δικαίωμα καὶ τοῦ κεκραγέναι με ἔτι πρὸς τὸν βασιλέα (what further *right* have I to cry to the king)

In this matter the translation reflects the Hebrew well:
ומה יש לי עוד צדקה ולזעק עוד אל המלך

This sense of δικαίωμα comes close to the meaning recorded for classical Greek by LSJ (*justification*), but it is better defined in the *ThDNT* with an example from Thuc I 41,1 δικαιώματα τάδε πρὸς ὑμᾶς ἔχομεν, referring to the established legal claims of allies. The meaning of δικαίωμα in 2 Kingdoms is determined on the basis of the Greek context as "justification."

"Greek words and Hebrew meanings"   85

The word is also used in a similar sense which we would define as "cause" or "case":

2Ch 6.35 καὶ ποιήσεις τὸ δικαίωμα αὐτῶν
([of God] and You will handle their case)
Je 18:19 εἰσάκουσον τῆς φωνῆς τοῦ δικαιώματός μου
(listen to the voice of my case)
Cp. also 11.20

This, in fact, is the only overlapping sense between the occurrences in the LXX and the general meanings of that word recorded in LSJ. The situation differs for the ThDNT and Walter Bauer's A Greek-English Lexicon of the N.T.[4], quoted here from the second English revision by Arndt-Gingrich-Danker (= BAGD). BAGD records the meanings of words for the N.T. and LXX only, and while doing so also gives parallels from other Greek works. The listing of these parallels in BAGD provides more background material for the usages of the LXX than the parallel entry in LSJ. The relevant entry in BAGD reads as follows:

1. *regulation, requirement, commandment* (so mostly LXX; Philo; Josephus; Cass. Dio (ii-iii A.D.; POxy 1119,15 τῶν ἐξαιρέτων τῆς ἡμετέρας πατρίδος δικαιωμάτων).
2. *righteous deed* (Arist. 1135a,12f; 1359a, 25; 1373b,1; 3 Km 3:28; Bar 2:19; N.T.).
3. [discussion of Ro 5:16 in the N.T.]

One obvious difference between the recording of LSJ and BAGD is that the meaning which apparently reflects the most frequent sense of δικαίωμα in the LXX (defined as "ordinance", "decree" in LSJ and as "regulation, requirement, commandment" in BAGD) is not documented outside the LXX according to LSJ, but is, according to BAGD, viz., in

Dio Cassius (ii-iii A.D.) and in POxy 1119 (254 A.D.).

[2,3] Another obvious difference between the two lexica is that BAGD (as well as *ThDNT*) adds a meaning "righteous deed" for which it provides support from Aristotle.

Our discussion will start from this latter meaning, not recorded by LSJ. There are three issues at stake:

1. Does a meaning "righteous deed" exist for the LXX, as claimed by BAGD?
2. Are there possibly two separate senses, "righteous deed", and "justice", both appearing in the LXX?
3. Is one of these senses, or possibly both, supported by external evidence?

Let us first review the evidence relating to the meanings "righteous deed" and "justice":

3Ki 3.28 φρόνησις θεοῦ ἐν αὐτῷ τοῦ ποιεῖν δικαίωμα (the wisdom of God was in him (sc. Solomon) to do justice / a righteous act)

Pr 8.20 ἐν ὁδοῖς δικαιοσύνης περιπατῶ, καὶ ἀνὰ μέσον τρίβων δικαιώματος ἀναστρέφομαι
(I walk in the ways of righteousness, and on the paths of justice I go about)

Pr 19.28 ὁ ἐγγυώμενος παῖδα ἄφρονα καθυβρίζει δικαίωμα, στόμα δὲ ἀσεβῶν καταπίεται κρίσεις
(he who answers for [?; becomes surety for] a foolish child insults justice and the mouth of the impious devours judgments)

In the latter two verses δικαίωμα has the sense of "justice" in general, as is especially clear from the words used in parallelism, δικαιοσύνη and κρίσις.

On the other hand, in 3Ki 3.28 δικαίωμα means either "justice" or "righteous act", as one of the manifestations of justice. Such a meaning is also evidenced for Bar 2.19, in the section of that book which has been translated from Hebrew (1.1 - 3.8).

Ba 2.19 ὅτι οὐκ ἐπὶ τὰ δικαιώματα τῶν πατέρων ἡμῶν ...
καταβάλλομεν τὸν ἔλεον ἡμῶν κατὰ πρόσωπόν σου
(for not by virtue of the righteous deeds of our ancestors ... do we present our supplication before you)

We thus conclude that the meanings "righteous act" and "justice" in a general sense are both evidenced for the LXX. Neither sense is listed in LSJ, but BAGD lists the first one, supporting this sense by evidence outside the LXX.

Returning to 3Ki 3.28, we note that the context favors the general meaning "justice" more than that of "righteous deed".

[4] Next we turn to the most frequently occurring meaning of δικαίωμα in the LXX. The reason for the high frequency of this use is related to the Hebrew source of the LXX and not any characteristic of the language of the LXX.

We refer to the meaning which is recorded as "ordinance", "decree" in LSJ and "regulation, requirement, commandment" in BAGD and which is or is not supported by external evidence. In most cases our only source for determining the meaning of the word is the Greek context of the LXX without relation to the Hebrew, but sometimes the Hebrew base text has to be involved as well.

Obviously, the act of determining the meanings of words in the LXX is very precarious, because the LXX is a translation, and it is often not clear to what extent the Hebrew text has to be invoked as well. The work of the LXX lexicographer is often that of an exegete of the LXX, and in the second place also of the Hebrew Bible.

Thus in order to determine the meaning of this δικαίωμα, we first note that this word is often used together with similar words in a long or short list:

Ge 26.5 καὶ ἐφύλαξεν τὰ προστάγματά μου καὶ τὰς ἐντολάς μου καὶ τὰ δικαιώματά μου καὶ τὰ νόμιμά μου
(and he kept my commandments and my orders and my ? and my laws)

The context does not enable us to determine the exact meaning of δικαίωμα, but the general sense is clear. In his conversation with Isaac, God mentions the various commandments which Abraham has fulfilled. Parallel to ἐντολή, νόμιμον, and πρόσταγμα, the word δικαίωμα probably indicates something issued by God, because the ἐντολαί and νόμιμα have been issued by God as well. According to the basic meaning of the root, δικαίωμα would thus mean something like a "just decree". On the other hand, δικαίωμα does not have to be intrinsically right or righteous, so that a neutral term such as "decree" or "ordinance" would cover the meaning better.

This feeling is corroborated by other verses:

Also in Ex 15.25, δικαίωμα, once again in plural, is given by God, in this case to Moses:

ἐκεῖ ἔθετο αὐτῷ δικαιώματα καὶ κρίσεις
(there He gave to him ? and judgments)

The word is also used not only in parallelism with the

"Greek words and Hebrew meanings"   89

mentioned words, but also in other close grammatical relationships:

Nu 30.17 ταῦτα τὰ δικαιώματα ὅσα ἐνετείλατο κύριος
(these are the ? which God ordered)
Nu 31.21 τοῦτο τὸ δικαίωμα τοῦ νόμου
(this is the ? of the law)

Summarizing, δικαίωμα thus often denotes some type of decree or ordinance given by God to men. The very use of the root δικ- could imply that every δικαίωμα is just or righteous, but this assumption is not necessary. Several of the usages of δικαίωμα outside the LXX are somehow connected with the legal world, without being intrinsically right. Therefore a neutral term such as "decree" or "ordinance" covers the Greek word well.

The fact that so far little evidence has turned up for this meaning outside the LXX may be coincidental. The translators used this word from Genesis onwards mainly for three Hebrew words, חֹק, חֻקָּה and מִשְׁפָּט; to be precise, 46 times for חק, 26 times for חקה, and 41 times for משפט. It also occurs 6 times for פְּקוּד, 3 times for צְדָקָה, and once each for דֶּרֶךְ, מִצְוָה, רִיב, צוּרָה, יָרִיב. Usually words of the Greek δικ- group reflect words of the Hebrew root צדק so that the equivalences of δικαίωμα, not related to this root, are interesting indeed. If we are allowed to generalize, we should say that the choice of δικαίωμα reflects a meaning common to both משפט and חקה / חק, viz., "decree". This sense of δικαίωμα is found also outside the LXX, even though not much evidence has turned up in support of this claim, and it is not mentioned in LSJ. Of the sources mentioned by BAGD, Philo and Josephus do not count, since they depend on the LXX. But two other sources do count. They are later than the LXX, but are not found in the realm of its influence, viz., Dio Cassius and the Oxyrrhynchus papyrus 1119 (254 A.D.): P Oxy 1119,15 τῶν ἐξαιρέτων τῆς ἡμετέρας πατρίδος δικαιωμάτων. Nevertheless *ThDNT* (without saying so explicitly), considers this sense as peculiar to the LXX, since it does not provide external evidence. Thus, the most frequent meaning of δικαίωμα in the LXX has presumably not been invented by the translators, but was found in their linguistic environment. It is therefore recorded as such in our sample entry (below).

Deliberations like these are relevant for the lexicographer since at one point he has to ask himself whether the difference between δικαίωμα and similar Greek words can be expressed lexicographically. In many languages it is often difficult to express such subtle nuances, especially when different authors use similar words in different ways. This applies also to the LXX which is far from consistent in this and other semantic realms. For example, D.W. Gooding (*The Account of the Tabernacle, Translation and Textual Problems of the Greek Exodus*, Texts and Studies, Second Series VI [Cambridge, 1959]) has noted the difficulties in the use of the cultic terms in Exodus. The inconsistencies regarding the use of the legal terms create similar difficulties which make it difficult to draw an exact dividing line between the different terms. In an article, written long ago, Sheldon Blank draws attention to these issues with regard to the semantic realm under investigation ("The LXX Renderings of Old Testament Terms for Law", *HUCA* 7 [1930] 259-283). He notes, for example, that different translators used δικαίωμα, πρόσταγμα and νόμιμον for חק and חקה. Thus, δικαίωμα is the preferred rendering for חקה and חק in the book of Deut, but in the remainder of the LXX it is either πρόσταγμα or νόμιμον. These differences between the various translators may have to be taken into consi-

"Greek words and Hebrew meanings"   91

deration in the lexicographical description, although preferably a lexicon of the LXX should try to avoid entering into the matter of the Hebrew equivalents. In our case, this information is probably less relevant, since δικαίωμα also frequently renders משפט.

The above is the analysis of this fourth sense of δικαίωμα. Since this is the most frequent sense of the word in the LXX, the lexicographer should attempt to describe some of the major aspects and usages of the word in the LXX.

Sometimes the word is used in the singular, but generally in the plural since the Hebrew Bible usually speaks about the ordinances of God in the plural.

In this sense, the word is almost always used in connection with God, so that it mainly refers to a divine decree. That is, there is nothing intrinsic in the meaning of δικαίωμα making it a divine decree, but the word is used in that way in the (Hebrew and) Greek Bible.

The δικαίωμα is usually given by God to men, or by Moses on his behalf:

Ex 21.1 καὶ ταῦτα τὰ δικαιώματα ἃ παραθήσεις ἐνώπιον αὐτῶν
(and these are the ordinances which you shall set before them)
A δικαίωμα can be accomplished, kept or fulfilled:

Le 25.18 καὶ ποιήσετε πάντα τὰ δικαιώματά μου
(and you shall do all my ordinances)
Δικαίωμα can be listened to, taught, and explained, the latter especially in the Wisdom psalms:

Ps 118(119).12 δίδαξόν με τὰ δικαιώματά σου
(teach me Your ordinances)

Most instances of δικαίωμα refer to the ordinances of the Israelites, but some to those of the gentiles:

4Ki 17.8 καὶ ἐπορεύθησαν τοῖς δικαιώμασιν τῶν ἐθνῶν
(and they walked in the ordinances of the nations)

The word is also used for the ordinances of the king (1Ki 8.9,11 etc; Mi 6.16).

Finally, since δικαίωμα often renders מִשְׁפָּט, it actually became one of the stereotyped renderings of that word. As such it was also used for meanings of that Hebrew word which are not covered by δικαίωμα; in other words, it also reflects hebraistic expansions of the semantic realm of the Greek word.

[5] = מִשְׁפָּט custom*(?), manner*(?)
1Ki 27.11 τάδε Δαυιδ ποιεῖ. Καὶ τόδε τὸ δικαίωμα αὐτοῦ πάσας τὰς ἡμέρας ἃς ἐκάθητο Δαυιδ ἐν ἀγρῷ τῶν ἀλλοφύλων
(these things David does. And this is [was] his מִשְׁפָּט = manner all the days when David dwelled in the land of the Philistines)

The translator of 1 Kingdoms atomistically represented מִשְׁפָּט with δικαίωμα, even though in this verse the Hebrew had a meaning different from its main sense. In my view, the best way of representing the meaning of this Greek word is to take it as a symbol for the Hebrew מִשְׁפָּט, here used as "custom", "manner". For a similar usage of δικαίωμα, see Ex 21.9,31.

Ex 21.9 κατὰ τὸ δικαίωμα τῶν θυγατέρων ποιήσει αὐτῇ
(according to the מִשְׁפָּט = manner (law?) of the girls he shall deal with her)

The assumption that this translation hebraistically

"Greek words and Hebrew meanings" 93

represents משפט would certainly hold if for this translator δικαίωμα would be the main rendering of משפט. However, even if this is not true, as in the case of Exodus, in which one finds an equal number of renderings of משפט with κρίσις, a similar reasoning holds, since the translator must have been influenced by the first verse in the chapter (21.1) starting with καὶ ταῦτα τὰ δικαιώματα ἃ παραθήσεις ἐνώπιον αὐτῶν. We therefore record this meaning as the hebraistic [5.] = משפט custom* (?), manner* (?).

ThDNT records Ex 21:9 as "the law of daughters", and likewise the next example (1Ki 2.13) as "the law of the priest". This stereotyped kind of recording may not be very helpful, though basically it is not incorrect. But it sounds awkward in English and therefore it highlights the problem under discussion. It is indeed very difficult to record in a modern lexicon the "meaning" of this δικαίωμα. One solution is to follow *ThDNT* and to record this word as "law". Another solution would be to record the word as "custom", "manner", but when doing so we would mislead the reader, since the translators did not have this sense in mind. When recording the word as "custom", "manner", we actually translate the sense of the Hebrew into English, assuming that a generation of readers of the LXX would detect the same meaning in δικαίωμα. What we propose to do is to take a middle course between these two types of recording, that is, between the use of "the law of the daughters", a meaning which the word probably never had in the Greek context and "custom", "manner", a meaning which the translators did not intend. For the translators δικαίωμα served merely as a symbol for משפט, so that the first meaning of this δικαίωμα is really משפט. To this recording we would add in English the specific sense of this δικαίωμα in the Greek context, which actually amounts to an English translation of משפט in the context.

This issue bears directly on the task of Septuagint lexicography in general. Do we record the meanings intended by the translators or do we record the meanings of the words as understood by the readers without reference to the translators? I think it would be difficult to exclude the intentions of the translators, for the task of the lexicographer is to record the meaning of the words in a text, in their context, and this can be determined only by relating those words to the intentions of the author. In our case the translator is the author. The first and main meaning of δικαίωμα is thus משפט, but it remains problematic to determine what we should write in English. This can be determined only on the basis of the context in Greek. The Greek could be taken as "custom", "manner", and with some difficulty also in general as "law". Because of these difficulties, we suggest a middle course as recorded here.

[6] =   משפט   *rightful due*(*)

1Ki 2.13 καὶ τὸ δικαίωμα τοῦ ἱερέως παρὰ τοῦ λαοῦ
(and the משפט = rightful due of the priest from the people)

The problem in understanding this meaning is similar to the preceding instance. The context is ambiguous. Of the known meanings of δικαίωμα, "decree" or "law" is hardly appropriate, since no decree or law is mentioned. We therefore record this sense as "rightful due" since in this context the priest receives something from the people. Once again we say, משפט is meant, a meaning which we would record as "rightful due". Whether or not to place an asterisk is difficult to decide as a similar meaning is evidenced in Modern Greek.

At the same time, cf. κρίσις in De 18.3 for a similar development: καὶ αὕτη ἡ κρίσις τῶν ἱερέων, τὰ παρὰ τοῦ λαοῦ ... καὶ δώσει τῷ ἱερεῖ ...

At the end of this analysis it should be stressed that the lexicographical description has to be as complete as possible, but does not have to cover solutions for all occurrences of a given word. As a rule, the description will not refer to doubts regarding the inclusion of a specific occurrence of δικαίωμα in either this or that meaning. On the other hand, the entry may refer in a footnote to specific occurrences, whose meanings are not comprehensible.

Thus I would add a note on:

Ho 13.1 κατὰ τὸν λόγον Εφραιμ δικαιώματα αὐτὸς ἔλαβεν ἐν τῷ Ισραηλ καὶ ἔθετο αὐτὰ τῇ Βααλ καὶ ἀπέθανεν
(according to the word [of?] Ephraim he took ?? in Israel and placed them for Baal and he died)

δικαιώματα reflects here רחת of MT, possibly read differently (Schleusner: רחות). It is hard to determine the meaning of δικαίωμα in this place, and in our view it should therefore not be mentioned in a lexicon.

A few annotated notes on the sources used for this analysis: LSJ, BAGD, MM, *ThDNT*, Schleusner, lexica for Modern Greek. Most helpful and relevant is BAGD. LSJ is of some help. Schleusner is of very little help, if at all. It is in fact not a lexicon, but a mere list of equivalents. *ThDNT* (H. Schrenk) is of some help, but at the same time it also misleads, since it lists separately δικαίωμα in the NT and outside the NT (including LXX), a distinction which is wrong since the use of words in the

NT often depends directly on that of the LXX. The LXX is now absorbed in the entry "δικαίωμα outside the NT". The correct subdivision should probably be: 1. so-called secular Greek, or Greek outside the biblical realm, 2. LXX, 3. NT.

Sample entry for a LXX lexicon

The asterisk indicates meanings which, according to the present state of knowledge, have been evidenced for the LXX only. The sequence reflects the logical order of the presumed development of the meanings. Meanings starting with a *Hebrew* word presumably developed hebraistically by expanding the semantic content of the Greek word on the basis of the Hebrew.

δικαίωμα

1. *legal right, justification* (2Ki 19.29); likewise: *legal case, cause* (2Ch 6.35 [of God] καὶ ποιήσεις τὸ δικαίωμα αὐτῶν; Je 18.19 εἰσάκουσον τῆς φωνῆς τοῦ δικαιώματός μου, cf. also 11.20).
2. *justice* (3Ki 3.28 τοῦ ποιεῖν δικαίωμα; τρίβων δικαιώματος // ὁδοῖς δικαιοσύνης Pr 8.20); cf. Modern Greek = "justice".
3. <=2a?> in plural: *righteous deeds* (Ba 2.19 τὰ δικαιώματα τῶν πατέρων αὐτῶν).
4. *decree(*), ordinance(*), regulation(*)* , sometimes in sg. (Nu 15.16; 27.11,etc), but usually in plural (Ge 26.5, Ex 15.25, etc.), almost always divine (Le 25.18, Nu 36.13, etc.), given by God (τίθημι [Ex 15.25], ἐντέλλομαι [Nu 30:17]), and kept by men (ποιέω [Le 25.18, De 6.24], φυλάσσω [De 6.2, 28.45 etc]) - used in

parallelism with ἐντολή, πρόσταγμα, νόμος and νόμιμον; usually of the Israelites (4Ki 17.19), but also of the gentiles (8: καὶ ἐπορεύθησαν τοῖς δικαιώμασιν τῶν ἐθνῶν [also 1Ma 1.13]); also used for the ordinances of the king (1Ki 8.9,11 etc).

5. = מִשְׁפָּט custom* (?), manner* (?) 1Ki 27.11, possibly also Ex 21.9 κατὰ τὸ δικαίωμα τῶν θυγατέρων ποιήσει αὐτῇ; 21.31.

6. = מִשְׁפָּט (rightful) due(*) (1Ki 2.13 καὶ τὸ δικαίωμα τοῦ ἱερέως παρὰ τοῦ λαοῦ; cf. κρίσις in De 18.3 for a similar development); cf. Modern Greek "dues", "fees" (J.T. Pring, The Oxford Dictionary of Modern Greek [Oxford, 1965]).

2. *The ὁμολογέω group*

Most of the words deriving from the stem ὁμολογ- in the LXX carry two basically different meanings. This situation differs from Classical Greek and has been created by the Hebrew. The double use is carried through in the NT and patristic literature.

We first turn to the basic meanings of the stem as recorded in the lexica. In some way or other the three basic meanings "to acknowledge/confess, promise, give thanks" are recorded in the various lexica. At the same time one should pay attention to the question whether the sense "to give thanks" is recorded as a separate sense or as a subsense of "to acknowledge", viz., "to acknowledge thanks".

LSJ

ὁμολογέω (Act.)
   I *agree with, say the same thing as*
   II 1. *correspond, agree with*
      2. *agree to, grant, concede, avow (gratitude), acknowledge, confess*
      3. *agree, promise to* (do)

ὁμολογία
   1. *agreement*
   2. *assent, admission, concession*
   3. *agreement, compact*
   4. *vow* [LXX Je 51(44).25 (pl.)]
   5. *conformity with nature*

ὁμολόγως
   1. *agreeably to, in unison with*
   2. *confessedly, openly*, LXX Ho 14.5; also ἐξ ὁμολόγου Plb. 3.91.10.

ἐξομολογέομαι
   1. *confess, admit, acknowledge,*
   2. *make grateful acknowledgements, give thanks, sing praises* (LXX, Philo, NT)

ἐξομολόγησις
      admission, confession, confession of gratitude
      Philo

ἀνθομολογέομαι
   I *make a mutual agreement*
   II 1. *confess freely and openly*
      2. *admit, signify*

"Greek words and Hebrew meanings" 99

3. *assent, agree*
4. *return thanks* (to God) LXX, NT, χάριν ἀνθ. Plut. Aem. 11

ἀνθομολόγησις
1. *mutual agreement*
2. *confession, admission, testimony*

BAGD
ὁμολογέω
1. *promise, assure*
2. *agree, admit*
3. *confess*
4. *declare (publicly), acknowledge, confess*
5. *praise* w. dat. Heb 13.15

ὁμολογία
1. act. *confessing* (as an action)
2. pass. *confession, acknowledgement* (that one makes)

ἐξομολογέω
1. act. *promise, consent*
2. mid. a. *confess, admit*
   b. *acknowledge*
   c. *praise* (deriving from mng. a [cf. Rtzst., Erlösungsmyst. 252])

MM
ὁμολογέω
agree with, acknowledge (+ parallels). '... With the usage "praise", "celebrate", in Heb 13.15, which Grimm-Thayer pronounces as "unknown to Grk. writ., "we may

compare the somewhat similar phrase ὁμολογῶ χάριτα in petitions, e.g. P. Ryl. II. 114³² (c. A.D. 280) ὅπως ... τῇ τύχῃ σου χάριτας ὁμολογεῖν δυνηθῶ, "that I may avow my gratitude to your fortune", P.Oxy. I.67²² (A.D. 338 ... χάριτας ὁμολογήσωμεν, and the Christian letter P.Oxy. VI.939⁶ (iv A.D.) ... ἡμᾶς χάριτας ὁμο[λογοῦντα]ς ...'; promise (+ parallels).

ὁμολογία
  contract, agreement (+ parallels)

ἐξομολογέω
  acknowledge, avow openly, consent, agree (+ parallels); 'In the LXX the idea of "give thanks", "praise", is prominent: cf. in the NT Mt 11.25, Lk 10.21, and perhaps Phil 2.11 (see Lightfoot ad loc.)."

ἀνθομολογέομαι
  agree, answer, acknowledge (+ parallels)

One of the main questions regarding the various usages of this word group is the background of the meaning recorded as "to give thanks". The distinctions between the various senses are admittedly very delicate. In any language, including Greek and Hebrew, the verbs "to confess" and "to give thanks" are two separate entities, but at the same time one has to ask the question whether the two groups are nevertheless somehow related. Is there a middle path in the Greek language which may be defined as "to acknowledge thanks" and which would explain the co-existence of these two senses? If that were true, the problem under discussion would be solved, since one would be able to see how one sense developed from the other. If we could find such a middle path in Biblical Hebrew, that

"Greek words and Hebrew meanings"   101

would only partially solve the problem, since what is possible in Hebrew is not necessarily possible in Greek. However, the issue is somewhat more complicated, and the question of the distribution of the word also comes into play.

First, then, the matter of the distribution of the senses.

The meanings "to agree, concede, acknowledge, confess, promise" are found in all of the Greek literature, including the LXX and the literature based on it. Some examples follow, referring to the simplex and its composita, both nouns and verbs:

Wi 18.13 ἐπὶ τῷ τῶν πρωτοτόκων ὀλέθρῳ ὡμολόγησαν θεοῦ υἱὸν λαὸν εἶναι (admit)
Si 4.26 μὴ αἰσχυνθῇς ὁμολογῆσαι ἐφ' ἁμαρτίαις σου (confess)
Je 44(51):25 ποιοῦσαι ποιήσομεν τὰς ὁμολογίας ἡμῶν ἃς ὡμολογήσαμεν (promise)
Da 9.20 ...καὶ ἐξομολογούμενος τὰς ἁμαρτίας μου (confess)

On the other hand, the meaning "to give thanks" is found only in the LXX and literature based on it, so that it is not impossible that this meaning has been created in the Hebrew realm. First some examples:

1Es 5.58 καὶ ἐφώνησαν δι' ὕμνων ὁμολογοῦντες τῷ κυρίῳ, ὅτι ...
                    (= הודה, give thanks)
1Es 9.8 δότε ὁμολογίαν δόξαν τῷ κυρίῳ ("thanks")
Ps 6.6 ἐν δὲ τῷ ᾅδῃ τίς ἐξομολογήσεταί σοι (= הודה, give thanks)
Ps 9.2 ἐξομολογήσομαί σοι Κύριε ἐν ὅλῃ καρδίᾳ μου διηγή-

σομαι πάντα τὰ θαυμάσιά σου (= הודה, give thanks)
Da 2.23 σοι, κύριε τῶν πατέρων μου, ἐξομολογοῦμαι καὶ αἰνῶ
לך אלהא אבהתי מְהוֹדֵא וּמְשַׁבַּח (= הודה, give thanks)

1Ch 25.3 ἐν κινύρᾳ ἀνακρουόμενοι ἐξομολόγησιν καὶ αἴνεσιν
τῷ κυρίῳ (= הודה, thanksgiving, thanks)
Ps 78(79).13 ἀνθομολογησόμεθά σοι εἰς τὸν αἰῶνα (= הודה, give thanks)

It is not easy to decide that a word or word group has been created or innovated by the LXX translators. Such decisions are based on the negative evidence of the extant Greek literature. However, if that evidence leads us to believe that a certain word looks like a neologism, a new creation, there always remains the possibility that it will turn up in a new papyrus or inscription. This has indeed been claimed for some uses of ὁμολογέω in the papyri. In our view these usages have been misinterpreted, as we shall see. It seems that there are still no parallels for the special use of ὁμολογέω in the LXX, and it is also not likely that these will ever turn up, as this use has presumably been determined by the Hebrew language.

In the light of the aforementioned examples it seems to us that the special use of the ὁμολογέω group in the LXX as "to give thanks" is sufficiently evidenced, both for nouns and verbs, the simplex and its two composita. It should however be added that in the lexica sometimes this use is also recorded as "to praise", but I do not think this is precise. We should adhere to the basic meaning "to give thanks", and if sometimes the word is used in parallelism with "to praise" that does not yet make ὁμολογέω to "praise" as well. This criticism applies to the dictionaries as well as to an article by J. Ledogar,

"Verbs of praise in the LXX translation of the Hebrew canon", *Biblica* 48 (1967) 29-56 who records ἐξομολογέομαι as "to praise" and therefore discusses this word together with the other words for praise in the LXX.

The sense "to give thanks" also occurs in the NT. For example:

Mt 11.25 ...ὁ Ἰησους εἶπεν, Ἐξομολογοῦμαί σοι, πάτερ κύριε τοῦ οὐρανοῦ καὶ τῆς γῆς = Lk 10:21

We now turn to the background of this special meaning. In our view this sense is not evidenced outside the realm of the LXX which includes the NT and other literary sources dependent upon it. This, however, is not accepted by all scholars. Several of them claim that the papyri contain an intermediary stage between the meanings "to confess" and "to thank", viz. χάριτας or χάριν ὁμολογεῖν, translated as "to acknowledge thanks". Such a use occurs, for example, in the following papyrus:

P. Ryl. II 114,32 (c. A.D. 280) ὅπως ... τῇ τύχῃ σου χάριτας ὁμολογεῖν δυνηθῶ

This approach is reflected, for example in MM, quoted above, and likewise in LSJ where one does not find a separate entry for ὁμολογέω as "to give thanks", but where that meaning is absorbed in sense II 2 (agree to, grant, concede, avow (gratitude), acknowledge, confess). For the sense "to avow gratitude" LSJ quotes the same papyrus as the lexicon of MM. However, there is some imprecision in this type of recording. Undoubtedly χάριτας or χάριν ὁμολογεῖν means "to avow gratitude", but that gratitude is expressed only by the noun, viz. χάριτας or χάριν, and not by the verb ὁμολογεῖν. Therefore the basic meaning of that verb remains unchanged by the usage of the papyri, viz., "to acknowledge", and no intermediary sense is detected.

Since there are no parallels for the sense "to give thanks" outside the LXX, we must try to locate the solution for the problem within the biblical realm. It seems to me that this meaning has developed from an etymological procedure which identified two Hebrew roots, י/ודה , "to confess" and י/ודה "to thank". In Hebrew these two senses are thus expressed by the same root. They are not homographs, since that would imply that they derived from different sources. Rather, these two verbs derived from a common source, or one sense developed from the other one. To find out the exact relation between the two senses of י/ודה as "to thank" and "to confess" is a matter for Hebrew linguists and exegetes. The fact remains that at this stage the senses usually appear as separate entities in the Bible. הודה in the Hiph'il is used generally as "to thank", but also a few times as "to confess", and התודה in the Hithpa'el is more frequently used as "to confess" than "to thank".

The translators, however, did not distinguish between these two basically different senses. They derived both of them from the meaning "to confess", and for this sense he used the Greek verb ὁμολογέω and compounds. This type of translation should be taken as a lack of recognition of a separate meaning "to give thanks". That is, when the translators should have used Greek verbs meaning "to give thanks" for Hebrew הודה, they used, instead, the Greek verb for "to confess".

In some way it is relevant to point to the closeness of the concepts of "givings thanks" and "confession". This can be strengthened by an analysis of some of the biblical texts. But it would be difficult to claim that the translators also made this link on a conceptual level, although that could have influenced the translators' decision. Therefore, I disagree with the theological approach explaining this rendering as "a Semitic linking of confessing sin and praising God", as has been done by *ThDNT* ad loc. Rather, the translators' decisions must have been based on an etymological procedure identifying the two verbs. This etymological approach is visible even in a few renderings of a word found outside the realm of "thanksgiving" and "confession", viz., הוד, glory, honor.

Ps 95.6 ἐξομολόγησις καὶ ὡραιότης ἐνώπιον αὐτοῦ
        (= תודה, thanksgiving)
    הוד והדר לפניו
    (RSV: Honour and majesty are before him)
Ps 103.1 ἐξομολόγησιν καὶ εὐπρέπειαν ἐνεδύσω
        (= תודה, thanksgiving)
    הוד והדר לבשת
    (RSV: Thou art clothed with honour and majesty)

These examples show that the translator of Psalms, who otherwise knows the meaning of the word הוד (cf. 20.6, 44.5, 144.5), derived the word in these two verses from the verbal form הודה, and used the usual equivalent for that word in the LXX. It is hard to know how this ἐξομολόγησις should be rendered into English;([1]) probably it would be best to say that the Greek word represents the Hebrew noun תודה, equated with "thanksgiving".

[([1]) Cf. the translation produced by the Holy Transfiguration Monastery in Boston, U.S.A., *The Psalter according to the Seventy of St. David, the Prophet and King* etc. (Boston, 1974): Ps 95.6 "Praise and beauty are before Him"; 103.1 "Confession and majesty hast Thou put on." Ed.]

The Greek translators thus used the ὁμολογέω group for various words and meanings of the Hebrew. It is not impossible that they themselves felt the difficulties involved, since for the meaning of "thanksgiving" the simplex is used much less than the composita ἐξομολογέομαι and ἀνθομολογέομαι. Possibly these two composita have been reserved for these special meanings.

The translation thus reflects the merging of two meanings in the wake of the Hebrew in a way which does not suit the Greek language. This is a true Hebraism which cannot be expressed well in a conventional lexicographical description of the LXX. The only way to express such a Hebraism would be to describe it as = הודה, to give thanks.

At the time of the translation there did not exist, in our view, a meaning "to give thanks", as the translators did not express such a meaning in their rendering. But such a sense for the group ἐξομολογέω was bound to develop. How else could a later generation explain a verse such as the following?

1Ch 25.3 ἐν κινύρᾳ ἀνακρουόμενοι ἐξομολόγησιν καὶ αἴνεσιν τῷ κυρίῳ (= תודה, thanksgiving, thanks)

In some verses somehow the sense "to confess" can be maintained, but the context makes such a claim impossible in this verse (as well as in 2Ki 22.50 = Ps 17.49; Ps 32.2). For the generation of the readers of the LXX thus there existed a new sense of ὁμολογέω, with its compounds, as "to thank", and the respective contexts made it easy for the readers to expand that meaning to the sense "praise", although this was not intended by the translators.

"Greek words and Hebrew meanings"

This new understanding of the Greek word has been expressed well in the anonymous Comm. Tura (Pap. Colon. Theol. 1) 5:13 on Ps 30.5: ἐξομολόγησις ἐνταῦθα οὐκ ἡ ἐξαγόρευσις ἐπὶ ἁμαρτήμασιν λέγεται. λέγεται μὲν γὰρ καὶ αὕτη ἐξομολόγησις ... ὡς ἐπὶ τὸ πλεῖστον οὖν ἐν τῇ γραφῇ ἡ ἐξομολόγησις διὰ τῆς λέξεως σημαίνεται ἡ εὐχαριστία.

But there remain problems, as illustrated by a quotation from Is 45.23 in Ro 14.11:

Is 45.23 κατ' ἐμαυτοῦ ὀμνύω ... ὅτι ἐμοὶ κάμψει πᾶν γόνυ καὶ ἐξομολογήσεται (S^c LC ὁμεῖται) πᾶσα γλῶσσα τῷ θεῷ (24 Δικαιοσύνη καὶ δόξα αὐτὸν ἥξουσιν)

בי נשבעתי ... כי לי תכרע כל ברך תשבע כל לשון

Ro 14.11 ζῶ ἐγώ, λέγει κύριος, ὅτι ἐμοὶ κάμψει πᾶν γόνυ καὶ πᾶσα γλῶσσα ἐξομολογήσεται τῷ θεῷ ⟨ἄρα οὖν ἕκαστος ἡμῶν περὶ ἑαυτοῦ λόγον δώσει τῷ θεῷ⟩
RSV:"...and every tongue shall give praise [or confess] to God"

It seems that within the context of the LXX the Greek verb has the meaning of "to give thanks", cf. the parallel phrase of the bowing of the knees. This is also clear from the continuation of the verse (24) λέγων Δικαιοσύνη καὶ δόξα πρὸς αὐτὸν ἥξουσιν. In Romans, however, the verse has been taken in a different sense. The continuation of the quotation ("so each of us shall give account of himself to God") makes it clear that Paul took the Greek as "to confess". This doubt regarding the meaning is further continued in the RSV in Romans where the word in the quote from Isaiah is translated as "give praise", but the note refers, more correctly, to "confess". Here, as elsewhere, the way in which NT quotations understand the words of the LXX cannot be taken as the only way of interpretation.

Finally, a lexicon does not have to explain all

occurrences of a given word. In the following two instances the meaning is not clear.

Ho 14.5 ἰάσομαι τὰς κατοικίας αὐτῶν ἀγαπήσω αὐτοὺς ὁμολόγως
ארפא משובתם אהבם נדבה
(RSV: I will heal their faithlessness; I will love them freely [=BDB])

In the translation, the use of the adverb ὁμολόγως is based on the rendering of נדבה, the voluntary offer, as ὁμολογία.

Job 8.21 τὰ δὲ χείλη αὐτῶν ἐξομολογήσεως
ושפתיך תרועה

Is the noun here used as "confession", "thanksgiving" or in a different sense?

SAMPLE ENTRIES

ὁμολογέω

1. *admit* + inf. Wi 18.13, 2Mc 6.6.
2. *confess* Est 1.1; ἐφ' ἁμαρτίας σου (Si 4.26), τὴν ἐπιθυμίαν αὐτῶν (Sus 14 θ '; cf. LXX ad loc. ἐξ-).
3. *promise* (or *vow** [cf. ὁμολογία Le 22.18]) Je 44(51).25.
4. = הודה (?) *give thanks** + dat. (to) σοί (IEs 4.60), τῷ κυρίῳ (5.58), abs. (Job 40.14)

→ ὁμολογία, ἐξ-, ἐξομολόγησις, ἀνθ-, ἀνθομολόγησις;

bibl. R.J. Ledogar, "Verbs of praise in the LXX translation of the Hebrew canon," *Biblica* 48 (1967) 29-56.

ὁμολογία

1. *promise* (or vow* [= נדר]) Le 22.18, Je 44(51).25.
2. *thanks*, δότε ὁμολογίαν δόξαν τῷ κυρίῳ (1Es 9.8).
3. = נדבה *voluntary offer** φέρω (De 12.6B), φάγω (12.17), ποιέω (Ez 46.12) (cf. ὁμολόγως = נדבה Ho 14.5); for a similar semantic development, cf. τὸ ἑκούσιον = נדבה *voluntary offer**.

ὁμολόγως

voluntarily ἀγαπήσω αὐτοὺς ὁμολόγως (Ho 14.5)

ἐξομολογέομαι

1. *confess* τὰς ἁμαρτίας μου (Da 9.4,20) τὴν ὀδύνην αὐτοῦ (Su 14; cf. θ' simplex)
2. = הודה (?) *give thanks** (often with musical instruments, Ps 32.2) usually + dat. (to), frequently in Ps, + σοι (6.6), + κυρίῳ (9.1), + τῷ ὀνόματί σου (53.6); + acc. τὰ θαυμάσιά σου Ps 88.5; + ἔναντι κυρίου (2Ch 7.6), ἐναντίον (Da 6.10[11]); abs. (2Ch 31.2); + ὅτι (Da 3.90); in 1-2Ch often paired with αἰνέω.

→ simplex

ἐξομολόγησις

1. = תודה *thanksgiving*,* *thanks*,* δίδωμι (Jo 7.19), // αἴνεσις (1Ch 25.3), ψαλμὸς εἰς ἐξομολόγησιν (Ps 99[100].1), all based on the etymological understanding reflected in ἐξομολογέομαι הודה - esp. visible in next usage; הוד = ('glory', but derived from הודה, as above)

thanks*, thanksgiving* ἐξομολόγησις καὶ ὡραιότης ἐνώπιον αὐτοῦ (Ps 95[96].6 thanksgiving and beauty*, before him), ἐξομολόγησιν καὶ εὐπρέπειαν ἐνεδύσω (103.1 'you have clothed yourself with thanksgiving and glory'), 148.13.

ἀνθομολογέομαι
1. *confess* 1Es 8.88, Si 20.3
2. = הודה (1) *give thanks* + dat. (Ps 78.13, Da 4.34); + εἰς (3Ma 6.33; ἐπί τινι).

ἀνθομολόγησις
1. = תודה *thanksgiving* 2Es 3.11, δίδωμι (Si 17.27).

3. ἐπιφανής

Neither LSJ nor MM refer to any special use of this word in the LXX.

<u>LSJ</u>
I 1. *coming to light, coming suddenly into view, appearing*
   2. of places and things: *in full view, visible*
   3. *manifest, evident*
II 1. *conspicuous, notable, distinguished, famous*
   2. *remarkable*
   3. *a title of divinities*

<u>AG</u>
   splendid, glorious

Thus, from the outset there appears to be no special LXX meaning for ἐπιφανής, whose general meanings are

"Greek words and Hebrew meanings"

"appearing", "visible", "evident", "famous" and "remarkable". We will, however, see that there are several complications for LXX lexicography. The meaning "evident", "visible" appears to be well-established in Pr 25.14:

ὥσπερ ἄνεμοι καὶ νέφη καὶ ὑετοὶ ἐπιφανέστατοι
(like winds and clouds and clearly visible rains)

This use is close to the etymology of ἐπιφανής, being derived from ἐπιφαίνω. In other places in the LXX the word is used as "glorious", another basic meaning of the Greek word, derived from its primary sense. Thus the Temple is "glorious" in 2Ma 14.33:

...καὶ ἱερὸν ἐνταῦθα τῷ Διονύσῳ ἐπιφανὲς ἀναστήσω

κύριος is glorious in 2-3Ma (e.g. 2Ma 15.34, 3Ma 5.35).

Also the "day of the Lord" in Jl 2.11 (cf. also 3.4) is described as "glorious":

διότι μεγάλη ἡ ἡμέρα τοῦ κυρίου, μεγάλη καὶ ἐπιφανὴς σφόδρα
Likewise, the "name" or "fame" of the people of Israel in 1Ch 17.21 is called "glorious":

...ὁ θεὸς ... τοῦ θέσθαι ἑαυτῷ ὄνομα μέγα καὶ ἐπιφανές

This applies also to the ὅρασις, that is, the "appearance", of the angel in Ju 13.6, both in MSS A and B:

Ju 13.6A ἄνθρωπος τοῦ θεοῦ ἦλθεν πρός με καὶ ἡ ὅρασις αὐτοῦ ὡς ὅρασις ἀγγέλου τοῦ θεοῦ ἐπιφανὴς σφόδρα
Ju 13.6B ἄνθρωπος θεοῦ ἦλθεν πρός με καὶ εἶδος αὐτοῦ ὡς

εἶδος ἀγγέλου θεοῦ φοβερὸν σφόδρα

The evidence thus seems to be uncomplicated. However, if one studies this word in the LXX more in detail, one realizes that the situation is more complex.

The different contexts indeed allow for an interpretation of the aforementioned instances of ἐπιφανής in the LXX as either "glorious", "evident" or "famous" and it seems to be methodologically sound to explain the word thus according to the natural meanings of the Greek word. As long as it is possible to explain words according to the Greek context, it is preferable that the lexicographer of the LXX be not influenced by the Hebrew text, but rather adheres to the Greek only.

However, often it is a mere ideal to resort only to the Greek context, forgetting that the LXX is a translation. Indeed, an analysis of Hb 1.7 shows that at least in this case the Hebrew should be consulted as well, and in the light of the mentioned difficulties encountered in this verse, the other verses actually have to be reassessed. Thus the aforementioned verses are, after all, not as uncomplicated as we thought beforehand.

Hb 1.7 (6 = τὸ ἔθνος τὸ πικρὸν ... τὸ πορευόμενον ἐπὶ τὰ πλάτη τῆς γῆς τοῦ κατακληρονομῆσαι σκηνώματα οὐκ αὐτοῦ) φοβερὸς καὶ ἐπιφανής ἐστιν (אָיֹם וְנוֹרָא הוּא)

In his description of the coming of the Chaldeans in 1.5-10 (11?), Habakkuk has little good to say about this people. They kill and destroy, they mock at the kings and there is "no end" to all of this. The people of the Chaldeans are described in the LXX of v. 7 as φοβερὸς καὶ ἐπιφανής. But what do these words mean? It is understandable why the Chaldeans should be called φοβερός, that is, "frightening", "terrible", but what does the next word, ἐπιφανής, mean in this context? Are the people called "conspicuous", "evident" or "famous"? After all, the Chaldeans are conspicuous and could be described as "famous", but neither of these words would fit the context. Or should we rather take ἐπιφανής as the opposite of its main meaning, that is, "infamous"? Such a meaning would very well fit the context, but is not evidenced for the Greek language.

The solution to the problem comes from a different corner, viz., the Hebrew text. It seems that the translator understood his text incorrectly, and that understanding gave rise to the present translation. The MT of Habakkuk described the Chaldeans as a frightful and terrible people: אים ונורא הוא, but the translator wrongly derived נורא from the root ראה, *to see*, and not from ירא, *to fear*. It does not really matter if we call this kind of etymology "wrong" or "idiosyncratic", but in any event it differs from the usual understanding of that word, and actually the confusion of these roots is known elsewhere in the textual and exegetical tradition of the Bible. Thus, instead of describing the people as "terrifying", the Greek translator described it as "visible". Reference to the Hebrew is here absolutely necessary in order to understand the background of the translation, because otherwise the Greek lexicographer may wish to ascribe to the word all kinds of hidden meanings, including "infamous". The mistakes of the translator are not of primary concern to the lexicographer of the LXX, nor does it matter for him if the Greek text makes sense – as long as the words themselves are understandable –, but in this case one needs to know what the translator had in mind before determining the meaning of this ἐπιφανής. It may not be very appropriate to say of the frightful people of the Chaldeans that they are "conspicuous". But this is how the translator took נורא. Thus ἐπιφανής should nevertheless be taken in its basic meaning as "conspicuous" regardless of the question whether or not such a meaning makes sense in the context. Accordingly, a LXX lexicon should nevertheless record this ἐπιφανής as another instance of "evident" or "conspicuous". Our knowledge that the use of this word in Hb 1.7 reflects a certain understanding of the Hebrew is thus not necessarily of interest for the Greek lexicographer, but nevertheless this information is used in the analysis.

In another case, in Ze 3:1 one is less certain about the meaning of the Greek word:

Ὦ ἡ ἐπιφανὴς καὶ ἀπολελυτρωμένη, ἡ πόλις ἡ περιστερά
(Alas the conspicuous [?] and redeemed city, the dove...)
הוֹי מֹרְאָה וְנִגְאָלָה הָעִיר הַיּוֹנָה
(RSV: "Woe to her that is rebellious and defiled, the oppressing city")

The context is that of a city in despair. It did not listen to the Lord, its leaders are corrupt and there is little good to say about that city. How should ἐπιφανής be taken in this context? Once again, one thinks at first about the city being "glorious". Obviously this is not very appropriate in the context, but the Greek word could still be taken as such if it be understood ironically. However, the Greek context warns one against ascribing exegetical inclinations to the translator. The verb גאל, used in MT as "defiled", is taken by the translator as derived from another meaning of that root, viz., "redeemed". And העיר היונה, "the oppressing city", has been misunderstood as "the city, the dove". This phrase makes in English as little sense as it does in Greek. Therefore, because in some details the translation makes little sense, from the outset it is not likely that ἐπιφανής reflects any special understanding of the context. As in the preceding example, the translator derived מראה from the root ראה, rendering it as if it were "visible" or the like. We should therefore take ἐπιφανής as "conspicuous", "visible", and not as "famous" because the translator did not have that meaning in mind.

It seems to us that also in other places translators derived נורא from the root ראה as if reading נראה, translating the word as ἐπιφανής. In fact, this also applies to the preceding examples which at first sight were considered uncomplicated. Thus the "day of the Lord" is likewise named ἐπιφανής (Jl 2.11, 3.4). But it is questionable to what extent the details of this thinking process of the translators are relevant for the lexicographer. For the Greek context in which "the day of the Lord" appears makes it more likely that it be described as "glorious" rather than the neutral "conspicuous". For example, in Jl 2.11 the only other descriptive adjective of the "day of the Lord" is μεγάλη and this applies also to Jl 3.4.

This applies also to the other cases. Certainly the appearance of the angel in Judith 13 described as נורא – ἐπιφανής reflects such an etymological understanding. The translator considered the word as "visible", but in the new, Greek, context, we have to take the word as "glorious".

It is actually remarkable that all instances of ἐπιφανής which do have a Hebrew equivalent reflect נורא. This applies also to other equivalents of this Greek root which has been more or less limited to the instances of נורא derived from ראה, *to see*.

For example,

2Ki 7.23 ולעשות לכם הגדולה ונֹרָאות לארצך
τοῦ ποιῆσαι μεγαλωσύνην καὶ ἐπιφάνειαν

Likewise, in Ze 2.11 נורא has been rendered with the verb ἐπιφαίνομαι.

Ze 2.11 נורא יהוה עליהם
ἐπιφανήσεται (many MSS: ἐπιφανὴς ἔσται) κύριος ἐπ' αὐτοὺς

In this latter case, too, ἐπιφαίνομαι is used in its regular meaning in Greek as "to appear", and actually it is of little concern to the Greek lexicographer how the translator arrived at this understanding. I might add that the Hebrew phrase stating that God is נורא "over" someone must have been difficult to some translators who preferred to see in it the root ראה. We should also add that this phrase need not be emended to נראה, as it occurs also elsewhere in the same way (Ps 66.5, 89.7, 96.4, etc.).

Returning to the meaning of ἐπιφανής in the quoted verses, we conclude that the translator apparently had an etymological conception in mind of נורא as נראה. In the light of this we could have explained also ἐπιφανής as "visible" or "conspicuous", but we did not let ourselves be influenced by this aspect of the use of the Greek word. Instead, we took the new, Greek, context into consideration. Thus, earlier the "appearance" of the angel of the Lord, depicted in the LXX as ἐπιφανής, was taken as "glorious" (Ju 13.6), and likewise we explained ἐπιφανής, used with regard to the "day of the Lord", as "famous" rather than "conspicuous".

Why, then, did we not invoke our knowledge of the translation procedure, but rather turned to the Greek context? It is hard to formulate any rules here. The main question is whether we should take the LXX as a Greek text or whether we should allow ourselves to be influenced by our conjectures on the translators' intentions. The rule of thumb we follow is that as long as possible we record the words of the LXX as if that text were a regular Greek text, explaining the words - conjecturally - in the way which a Greek reader would have taken them. After all, that is the task of the lexicographer of any text. Only when this procedure would lead to unrealistic results, when no feasible meaning can be derived from the Greek context, our knowledge about the translators' intentions is invoked. In other words, as long as possible, ἐπιφανής is explained according to its Greek context as either "conspicuous" or "famous", etc., even when our analysis of the translation makes it likely that the translator had a different meaning in mind. However, when no feasible meaning can be derived from the Greek context, our knowledge of these intentions is invoked. These difficulties should, in our view, be recorded in the individual entries in a lexicon.

In an appendix to this analysis, let us turn to the use of ἐπιφανής in the NT. It occurs only once, in Ac 2.20, in a quotation from Jl 3:4, that is, the aforementioned verse about the "day of the Lord". It is very tempting to connect this word with the specific meaning of ἐπιφάνεια in the NT referring to the "epiphany", the manifestation, or appearance of God or Christ. One recent scholar indeed suggested that this ἐπιφανής in Acts reflects "terminology used of the Hellenistic monarchs (and subsequently in the Roman Imperial cult) being applied to God. The implication of the presence of the word in Peter's Pentecost speech is to suggest Jesus' divinity, as the following verses more explicitly indicate (Ac 2.22,36)". (G.H.R. Horsley, *New Documents*, vol. 4 [Sydney, 1987], 148). However, the context does not use ἐπιφανής or ἐπιφαίνομαι or a similar or parallel word with regard to Jesus, nor is Jesus' appearance stressed in these verses. The next verses make it clear that the text of Zephaniah was quoted in order to show that the wonders which Jesus performed were foretold by Joel. In our view, in the case of quotations from the LXX in the NT, as a rule the meanings of the words in these quotations should be taken in exactly the same way as they appear in the LXX, so that the verse in Acts actually does not add any new dimension to the aforementioned analysis of ἐπιφανής in the LXX.

The sample entry for a LXX lexicon thus reads:

1. *evident* ἄνεμοι καὶ νέφη καὶ ὑετοί (Pr 25.14), *conspicuous* τὸ ἔθνος (Hb 1.7), πόλις (Ze 3.1).
2. *glorious* ἱερόν (2Ma 14.33), κύριος (15.43, 3Ma 5.35), ἡ ἡμέρα τοῦ κυρίου (Jl 2.11, 3.4), ὄνομα (1Ch 17.21), ὅρασις (Ju 13.6).

N.B. Exact distinction between these two meanings is often not possible when the translation reflects etymological exegesis of נורא (and sim.) from ראה.

4. ὀρθρίζω

The verb ὀρθρίζω does not create any specific difficulties in the Greek language in which, incidentally, it occurs rarely. Only in the literature which is somehow related to Hebrew sources do some problems arise.

"Greek words and Hebrew meanings"   119

Two different forms are used in Greek, ὀρθρεύω, the Attic form, and ὀρθρίζω used in the LXX and NT, as well as in the literature dependent on these sources and, in a different form, as ὀρθρίζω and ὀρτίζω in an ostracon and a papyrus. The entry in LSJ gives little information, but the Supplement provides a detailed entry with three different meanings.

LSJ
= ὀρθρεύω, LXX Ev. Luc. 21.38

ὀρθρεύω, (ὄρθρος) *lie awake before dawn*, Theocritus, Eur.; ὀρθρεύεσθαι καλοῦσιν οἱ 'Αττικοὶ τῷ λύχνῳ προσκεῖσθαι, πρὶν ἡμέραν γενέσθαι, Phryn. PS p. 93 B

LSJ Suppl.
1a (=Attic ὀρθρεύω, Moer. p. 272 P) *rise up early*, LXX Ge 19.2, Ps 126(127).2.
b metaph., *be eager or earnest*, ὀρθρίζων Je 25.3
2 *go early*, εἰς τόπον ib. Ge 19.27; *go eagerly or earnestly*, πρός τινα ib. Ps 62(63).2, Si 39.5, Ev.Luc. 21.38
3 προῆγεν ὀρθρίζων καὶ ὀψίζων at morning and evening Thd 1Ki 17.16

AG
(Moeris p. 272 ὀρθρεύει 'Αττικῶς, ὀρθρίζει 'Ελληνικῶς) impf. ὤρθριζον *bc up or get up very early in the morning* ... ὁ λαὸς ὤρθριζεν πρὸς αὐτὸν ἐν τῷ ἱερῷ ἀκούειν αὐτοῦ *the people used to get up very early in the morning* (to come) *to him in the temple and hear him* Lk 21.38 (ὀρ. πρός τινα also means gener. *seek someone diligently*: Job 8.5; Ps 77.34; Si 4.12; Wi 6.14; Test Jos 3.6)

MM

... According to Thumb (*Hellen.*, p. 123) the dependence of the verb on the Heb. השכים in the sense of 'rise early' is very improbable, and reference is made to such analogous verbs in M Gr as νυχτορεύω 'work throughout the night,' and μεσημεριάζω 'do something at midday.'

The meaning "to get up early in the morning" is the basic sense of this verb and as such it occurs also in various places in the LXX. As a rule it reflects the root שכם in the Hiph'il, usually in the form וישכם, that is "and he got up early in the morning", often linked pleonastically with בבקר. For example,

Ju 21.4 AB καὶ ἐγένετο (A: ἐν) τῇ ἐπαύριον καὶ ὤρθρισεν ὁ λαός
ויהי ממחרת וישכימו העם
Ge 19.27 ὤρθρισεν δὲ Αβρααμ τὸ πρωί.
וישכם אברהם בבקר
Ex 34.4 καὶ ὀρθρίσας Μωυσῆς ἀνέβη εἰς τὸ ὄρος τὸ Σινα
וישכם משה בבקר ויעל אל הר סיני
Ps 62.2 Ὁ θεὸς ὁ θεός μου, πρὸς σὲ ὀρθρίζω
(God, my God, for thee I get up early in the morning)
אלהים אלי אתה אֲשַׁחֲרֶךָּ
(RSV: O God, thou art my God, I seek thee)
Is 26.9 ἐν νυκτὸς ὀρθρίζει τὸ πνεῦμά μου πρὸς σέ, ὁ θεός
בלילה אף רוחי אליך אֲשַׁחֲרֶךָּ
(RSV: My soul yearns for thee in the night)
Ho 5.15 ἐν θλίψει αὐτῶν ὀρθριοῦσι πρός με λέγοντες
בצר להם יְשַׁחֲרֻנְנִי
(RSV: and in their distress they seek me)

Once again we enter into problems of Hebrew etymology. For in the three last mentioned examples (Ps, Is and Ho), the Hebrew text uses the verb שׁחר, to *seek*, but the Greek translators derived these forms from the noun שׁחר, *morning*. However, as in the example of ἐπιφανής, it is not necessarily the task of the Greek lexicographer to trace the background of this Hebrew-Greek etymologizing rendering, but rather to understand the Greek word in its context. Indeed, the resulting translation, referring, like שׁחר, to the "morning", is quite possible. Thus, instead of the verb of the Hebrew text which should be taken as "to seek earnestly, diligently", the LXX uses here ὀρθρίζω, which I take as "to get up early in the morning" for someone. These two verbs are quite different, so that we read, e.g., in the LXX of Ps. 62.2 "My God, My God, early in the morning I get up for thee" instead of MT "O God, thou art my God, I seek thee". In my view, in spite of the Hebrew, in these verses the basic meaning of the Greek verb has not changed. The resulting translation simply differs from MT. The Greek verb is used in a way slightly different from its use in classical Greek, namely not as just "to get up early", but as "to get up early for someone". This particular use is created by the etymological rendering of the verb שִׁחֵר from שַׁחַר, *morning*. Accordingly, there is no need to ascribe to the Greek verb a new meaning such as in BAGD ("seek someone diligently") or in *New Documents*, vol. 1 (Sydney, 1981), p. 86 ("to come"). These sources thus adapt the meaning of the Greek verb to the context, more specifically, BAGD ascribes to ὀρθρίζω the meaning of its Hebrew counterpart, a procedure which is quite questionable from a methodological point of view.

This use of ὀρθρίζω with a preposition is possible in

Greek, as is shown by the text of the Amsterdam ostracon, discussed at some length in *New Documents*, vol. 1, p. 86: ἵνα μίνῃς αὐτόν, ἐπὶ γὰρ ὀρτίζει πρός σε αὔριον (22.7-8 [II]). In that ostracon there appears to be a misspelling (omission of the ρ), also known from the MSS of the LXX (in Ps. 126.2 Codex S has ὀρθίζω), but nevertheless it is quite clear that ὀρθρίζω is meant in the Amsterdam ostracon. I do not think that in any of these places the original meaning of the Greek, that is "to go early" or "to rise early" has been lost, and in any event it would be hard to prove such an assumption. A comparison with these documents, then, shows that in the use of the verb with a preposition no Hebraism is involved since a similar construction is found in two external sources not dependent on the LXX (O. Amst. 22 7-8 (ii A.D.) and P. Mil. Vogl. II 50.13 (I) πορεύου οὖν ὀρθίσας εἰς (so rising up early, go to...).

The verb occurs also once in Luke: ὁ λαὸς ὤρθρισεν πρὸς αὐτὸν ἐν τῷ ἱερῷ ἀκούειν αὐτοῦ (21:38), which I would translate as "The people rose up early in the morning to (see) him in the temple", or, as in the RSV, "And early in the morning all the people came to him in the temple". The use of the verb in Luke follows the usage of the LXX, as so often elsewhere in that book, but since this usage is also found outside the LXX, Luke's dependence on the LXX cannot be proven.

So far we have covered one of the two senses of ὀρθρίζω, subdivided differently by the lexica. In our own sample entry the data are as following:

1. *get up early in the morning* (cf. ὄρθρος) Ju 21.4, 1Ki 5.3, To 9.6, usually pleonastically joined with τὸ πρωί

(following MT בבקר השכים) Ge 19.27, 20.8, Ex 24.4; often the participle is used together with other verbs ὀρθρίσας δὲ Μωυσῆς τὸ πρωὶ ᾠκοδόμησεν θυσιαστήριον (Ex 24.4), καὶ ὀρθρίσας 'Ιησοῦς τὸ πρωὶ ἐπεσκέψατο τὸν λαόν (Jo 8.10); also with verbs of motion καὶ ὀρθρίσας Μωυσῆς ἀνέβη εἰς τὸ ὄρος τὸ Σινα (Ex 34.4), καὶ ὀρθρίσαντες τὸ πρωὶ ἀνέβησαν εἰς τὴν κορυφὴν τοῦ ὄρους (Nu 14.40); abs. with εἰς *get up early in the morning (and go) to* ὤρθρισεν δὲ Αβρααμ τὸ πρωὶ εἰς τὸν τόπον (Ge 19.27), ὀρθριεῖτε αὔριον εἰς τὴν ὁδὸν ὑμῶν (Jd 19.9), with ἐν: καὶ ὀρθρίσατε ἐν τῇ ὁδῷ (1Ki 29.10); πρός τινα *get up early for someone* (God) Ό θεὸς ὁ θεός μου, πρὸς σὲ ὀρθρίζω (Ps 62[63].2), ἐκ νυκτὸς ὀρθρίζει τὸ πνεῦμά μου πρὸς σέ, ὁ θεός (Is 26.9), ἐν θλίψει αὐτῶν ὀρθριοῦσι πρός με λέγοντες (Ho 5.15) (in all these cases, as well as in Job 8.5, Ps 77[78].34, an aspect of yearning is extant in the Hebrew verb [שחר, *to seek*], but not necessarily in the Greek verb where this aspect is expressed by the preposition). Cf. O. Amst. 22.7-8(II) ἵνα μίνῃς αὐτόν, ἐπὶ γὰρ ὀρτίζει πρός σε αὔριον and the discussion in *New Documents* 1, p. 86.

The sense listed as the third one in LSJ (ὀρθρίζων = "at morning") is not distinct from the other ones and should, in my view, be listed together with them.

But there is one other sense ("early", "earnestly") listed as **1.b** in LSJ and as a separate meaning **2** in my own sample entry which relates to the problem of the understanding of the Hebrew and should be taken as a Hebraism.

2Ch 36.15 καὶ ἐξαπέστειλεν κύριος ... ὀρθρίζων καὶ ἀποστέλλων τοὺς ἀγγέλους αὐτοῦ
(and the Lord sent... his messengers ? and sending)
וישלח יהוה ... ביד מלאכיו השכם ושלוח

Je 25.3 ἐλάλησα (sc. κύριος) πρὸς ὑμᾶς ὀρθρίζων καὶ λέγων
(I [that is, the Lord] spoke to you rising up [?] and saying)

ואדבר אליכם אשכים ודבר

ib. 4 καὶ ἀπέστελλον πρὸς ὑμᾶς τοὺς δούλους μου τοὺς
προφήτας ὄρθρου ἀποστέλλων

ושלח יהוה אליכם את כל עבדיו הנבאים השכם ושלח

This ὀρθρίζων has been recorded here as "השכם = early, earnestly*" with the following implication: The construction in which ὀρθρίζων occurs twice differs from that of the other instances, and it is used so ungrammatically that we can only say that it represents the adverb השכם hebraistically. In 2Ch 36.15 it cannot be taken as "to get up early" as that use would not fit the subject, the Lord. It is not clear how the Greek should be translated: and the Lord sent... his messengers rising up early (?) and sending?. Moreover, the participle ἀποστέλλων is awkward as it is identical with the main verb. This applies also to the verse in Jeremiah. From the continuation of the verse (v. 4) we understand how ὀρθρίζων is to be taken. It is apparently used as if it were an adverb, just as in the Hebrew, and parallel to v. 4, where the Greek text renders the exactly same phrase השכם ושלוח with an adverb ὄρθρου ἀποστέλλων, sending early in the morning.

In these two verses ὀρθρίζων is thus used ungrammatically and hebraistically, and the only way in which this word can be taken is as an exact equivalent of השכם, so to speak as a symbol for it. Lacking any better system, the real meaning of this ὀρθρίζων is thus השכם, which should then be rendered into English as both "early" and "earnestly". It should be rendered as "early" because that is the etymologically correct meaning. At the same time it should be rendered as "earnestly" because the Hebrew as

"Greek words and Hebrew meanings"   125

well as the Greek word seem to be used in this way, and certainly the Greek reader will understand the implication to be "earnestly", even if he does not understand exactly how the Greek word developed in that direction. "A Greek word with a Hebrew meaning", to use the title of the book by D. Hill.
The second part of the sample entry thus reads:

2. ὀρθρίζων = השכם early, earnestly*, of the sending of God's message to mankind, used ungrammatically as a participle (// ὄρθρου used in the same situations) καὶ ἐξαπέστειλεν κύριος ... ὀρθρίζων καὶ ἀποστέλλων τοὺς ἀγγέλους αὐτοῦ (2Ch 36.15), ἐλάλησα (sc. κύριος) πρὸς ὑμᾶς ὀρθρίζων καὶ λέγων (Je 25.3, cf. v. 4: καὶ ἀπέστελλον πρὸς ὑμᾶς τοὺς δούλους μου τοὺς προφήτας ὄρθρου ἀποστέλλων).

INDEXES

(1) Index of Passages
   [Only those passages on which there is a substantial discussion are listed.]

Genesis = Ge
19.27	119
29.20	64
37.4	65
40.4	6

Exodus = Ex
34.4	123

Leviticus = Le
5.13	46
15.3	12f.

Numbers = Nu
27.23	11
32.28	11

2Kingdoms = 2Ki
7.23	116
19.29	84

1Chronicles = 1Ch
25.3	102,106,109
17.21	118

2Chronicles = 2Ch
6.35	85
36.15	123

Judith = Ju
13.6	111
21.4	120

Job
8.21	108
15.32	9

Psalms = Ps
30.5	107
62.2	121
95.6	105
103.1	105
117.27	8ff.

Proverbs = Pr
4.6	70
7.18	72
8.17	70
8.21	71
8.36	73
20.13	69
21.17	71
25.14	111
29.3	71
30.15	69
30.16	72

Hosea = Ho
14.9	9
5.15	120
14.5	98,108

Joel = Jl
2.11	111,118
3.4	111,118

Indexes

Obadaiah = Ob
1   47

Habakkuk = Hb
1.7   112

Zephaniah = Ze
2.11   116
3.1   118

Malachi = Ma
3.9   45

Isaiah = Is
26.9   123
45.23   107
56.10   68

Jeremiah = Je
18.19   85
25.3   124
25.4   124

2Maccabees = 2Ma
14.33   111
15.34   111

3Maccabees = 3Ma
5.35   111

Luke = Lk
21.38   119

Acts = Ac
2.20   117

Romans = Ro
14.11   107

Apollodorus Mythographus
3.14.6   10

Aristotle
Rhet. 1371ª 21   53
Eth.Nic. 1126ᵇ 22   54

Archilochus
25.3   70

Dionysius of Halicarnassus
Ant. Rom. 8.34   59

Philo
Spec. Leg. 2.258   71

Plato
Theages, 122a   7

Plotinus
2.9.16   59

Plutarch
Per. 1   54

Xenophon
Mem. 2.7.9,12   53

Pap. Colon. Theol. 1
5.13   107

P. Ryl. II
114.32   100

O. Amst.
22.7-8   122

Indexes

(2) Index of Greek Words

ἀγαπάω	77-79
ἀγάπη	51f,80
ἀγάπησις	58,79
ἀγαπητός	64,67,70,81
ἀναβαίνω	40
ἀνθομολογέομαι	98,100,106,110
ἀνθομολόγησις	99,110
ἀποβλέπω	45f
βλέπω	36
γινώσκω	26f
δικαίωμα	x,83-97
δουλεύω	30,35
δοῦλος	35f
δύναμαι	38f
δῶρον	46
ἕκαστος	19f
ἐκεῖνος	39
ἐντολή	88
ἐξαποστέλλω	28f
ἐξαίρω	31f
ἐξομολογέομαι	98,109
ἐξομολογέω	99,100
ἐξομολόγησις	98,109
ἑορτή	9
ἐπιφαίνομαι	116
ἐπιφανής	110-118,121
ἐράω	70
ἔρχομαι	34
ἔρως	51f,72
ἕως	20f
ἤ	21-23
ἥκω	34f
θυσία	46f
θυσιαστήριον	46
ἰσχύς	41f
καθίστημι	12

κατακληρονομέω	43f
καταφιλέω	65
κεφάλη	28
κληρονομέω	44
κυνέω	58
κύω	58
μή	23f
νόμιμον	88
ὁμολογέω	97-110
ὁμολογία	99,100
ὁμολόγως	98,109
ὅρασις	111
ὁράω	36f
ὀρθρεύω	119
ὀρθρίζω	118-25
περιοχή	47
πυκάζω	8f
στέργω	50 et passim
συνίστημι	1-15
φιλέω	48 et passim
φιλία	51
φίλος	56
φιλοσοφέω	71
φιλοσοφία	71
ψυχή	42f

(3) <u>Index of Hebrew Words</u>

אהב Qal	51,62,63,65,75
אַהֲבָה	64
אָהֲבִים	72
אסר Qal	10
גאל Nif.	114
דֶּרֶךְ	89
חֹק	89,90
חֻקָּה	89,90
ידה Hif.	104-110

יָדִיד		64
יָרִיב		89
יָרֵא "fear"		113
יְשֻׁרוּן		64
מִזְבֵּחַ		46
מִנְחָה		46
מִצְוָה		89
מִשְׁפָּט		89-97
נְדָבָה		108
נוֹרָא		113
נשק	Qal	64
עָבֹת		9
עמד	Qal	14
פִּקּוּד		89
צוּרָה		89
קנה	Qal	69
ראה	Nif.	113-17
רחם	Pu.	69
רִיב		89
רְתֵת		95
שחר	Qal	121
שַׁחַר		121
שכם	Hif.	120,124f
שמר	Qal	69
תּוֹרָה		106

(4) **Index of Modern Authors**

[On BAGD, BDB, BDF, KB, LSJ, and MM, see the list of abbreviations on pp. xv-xvi.]

Anz, H.	12n
BAGD,	2,18n,22,24.60n,64,71,85,86,87,89 95,99,121
Barclay, W.	50,51n,54n,59n
Barr, J.	51n,55n,61n,62n,75n
Barthélemy, D.	61n
Bauer,W.	18n

BDB	8,11,18n
BDF	22,23,24,36,38,39
Blank, Sh.	90
Brenton, L.C.L.	8,9,14
Briggs, Ch.A.	11n
Briggs, E.G.	11n
Brock, S.P.	vi,61n,75n
Bromiley, G.W.	52n
Bultmann, R.	27
Caird, G.B.	50n
Conybeare, F.C.	8
Ceresa-Gastaldo, A.	74n
Cox, C.E.	ix,xiv
Cross, F.M.	viii
Dalman, G.	44
Daniel, S.	46n
Davies, W.D.	50n
Dorival, G.	37n,45n
Driver, S.R.	18
Eisenbeis, W.	vii
Foerster, W.	44
Ford, D.	xiv
Fox, G.	ix
Fries, C.C.	17n
Fritsch, C.T.	vii
Gilliéron	58n
Glare, P.G.W.	26,26n
Gooding, D.W.	90
Goshen-Gottstein, M.H.	viii
Hamerton-Kelly, R.	50
Hanhart, R.	viii
Harl, M.	37n,42n
Hatch, E.	2,17,67n,72n
Heinen, H.	36
Helbing, R.	31,36
Hill, D.	83
Hogg, C.F.	65,66,n
Horsley, G.H.R.	118

Jacques, X.	33,61n	
Jarick, J.	44n	
Jellicoe, S.	vi,61n,69n	
Jenkins, R.G.	ix	
Joly, R.	xii,53n,55ff,55n*bis*,56n*bis*,57n*quatt*	
	58n,59n*bis*,61n,66n,74n	
KB	11	
Kiessling, E.	2	
Kittel, G.	27,35,44	
Klein, R.W.	48n	
Kraft, R.A.	vii*tert*,viii*bi*,61n,62n,63n	
Langenscheidt,	25	
Ledogar, J.	102,109	
Lee, J.A.L.	viii,ix,x*bis*,1-15,29,37n,55n,61n	
	62n,63n,73n	
Lewis, Ch.T.	25	
LSJ	1*bis*,2*tert*,6,8*tert*,9*bis*,10,11	
	12*bis*,13,14,15 28,29,53,54,n*bis*,	
	60n*bis*,64,65n*bis*,67n,68n, 72n*bis*,79,	
	83,84*bis*,85*quinq*,86,87*bis*,89,95*bis*	
	98,103*bis*,110*bis*,119*tert*,123*bis*	
Lyons, J.	33n	
Margolis, M.L.	22	
Mayser, E.	36,38*bis*,39*bis*	
MM	40,95,103*bis*	
Munnich, O.	37n	
Muraoka, T.	ix*bis*,17-47	
Muses, C.A.	8	
Olley, J.W.	x	
Orlinsky, H.M.	61n	
Preisigke, F.	2,40,41	
Pring, J.T.	97	
Pusey, E.	45n	
Quell, G.	51n	
Rabin, C.	61n	
Rahlfs, A.	2*bis*,13,49n*bis*	
Redpath, H.A.	2,17,20n,32,67n,72n	
Rengstorf, K.H.	35	
Saussure, F. de	33	

Schleusner, J.F.	2,6,8*bis*,14*bis*,15,19*bis*,n,23,31
	95*tert*
Schort, Ch.	26
Schrenk, H.	95
Scroggs, R.	50n
Shipp, G.P.	58n
Silva, M.	30n
Soisalon-Soininen, I.	24
Spicq, C.	55n
Sprenger, H.N.	45n
Stauffer, E.	51,n,53,n
Stock, St G.	8
Sweet, H.	17n
Swete, H.B.	61n
Swinn, S.P.	ix,xii,49-81
Tarelli, C.C.	52n*bis*,53n,56n
Thackeray, H.St J.	35,62n,63n,68n,72n
Thomson, A.	8
Tov, E.	viii*bis*,ix*bis*,x*bis*,xiii*quinq*,37n
	83-125
Turner, G.A.	51,52n
Walters, P.	36
Warfield, B.	56n
Wevers, J.W.	viii,13

www.ingramcontent.com/pod-product-compliance
Lightning Source LLC
Chambersburg PA
CBHW032259150426
43195CB00008BA/516